▲▲ ▲ ▲▲ ▲ ▲▲ ▲ ▲▲ ▲ **Nan** ▲▲ ▲ ▲▲ ▲ ▲▲ ▲ ▲▲ ▲

Living Large

▲ ▲ ▲

Caroline Speare Rohland, Wilna and Nan
at the Window. *At home in Bearsville, New
York, and seated at their favorite window on
a winter afternoon, the two artists (Nan at
left, Wilna on the right) look out at the snow-
covered grounds and watch the birds at the
several feeders Nan had built. A lifelong friend
and confidante of Wilna and Nan, Rohland
captured the cozy atmosphere of their home and
the warmth of their enduring relationship.*

Living Large

Wilna Hervey and Nan Mason

▲▲▲

JOSEPH P. ECKHARDT

WoodstockArts

Woodstock, New York

Related titles available from WoodstockArts:

Woodstock History and Hearsay (second "art book" edition), by Anita M. Smith

Under the North Light: The Life and Work of Maud and Miska Petersham, by Lawrence Webster

10 9 8 7 5 5 4 3 2

WoodstockArts
P.O. Box 1342
Woodstock, New York 12498
Tel: 845-679-8111
F: 419-793-3452

Info@WoodstockArts.com
www.WoodstockArts.com

Cataloging-in-Publication (CIP) Data
Eckhardt, Joseph P., 1944-
      Living large : Wilna Hervey and Nan Mason / Joseph P. Eckhardt. Woodstock, NY : WoodstockArts, 2015.
200 p. : cm.
      Includes bibliographical references.
   ISBN-10: 0-9679-2688-2
   ISBN-13: 978-0-9679-2688-9   2014954153
      1. Women artists--United States—Biography. I. Title

      CT 3200 .E35
920 Her

WoodstockArts would like to thank Amy Booth Raff,
of the Woodstock Library, for the CIP data.

Book design by Abigail Sturges

Printed in China

Contents

Introducing
Wilna and Nan

When Wilna Hervey began her brief movie career in 1916, she never dreamed that the story of her life would take on more surprising twists and turns than the plots of the silent comedies she was making. Nor did she suspect for a moment that the co-star of her life's scenario would be another woman.

Graduating from high school in the Bronx in 1914, Nan Mason planned to take some secretarial courses, get married and settle down to raise a family. Had someone predicted then that she would instead become an artist, and end up living most of her life with a former silent-film star who stood six-foot-three and tipped the scales at three hundred and fifty pounds, Nan would have laughed her famously loud and raucous laugh and enjoyed the outrageous joke.

And yet a long, full and remarkably happy life together was precisely what fate had in store for these two young women. Although born at opposite ends of the country in families of substantially different economic and social circumstances, they met in 1920 when Wilna made a series of comedy films with Nan's father, a noted character actor. That fortuitous encounter led to an unexpected and passionate friendship of a sort that neither girl had ever experienced. A fateful decision in 1924, to spend their lives together in mutual pursuit of art, brought the young couple to a fabled art colony in the Catskills where they would live the rest of their lives.

The home of writers, painters, sculptors and musicians for more than a century, Woodstock, New York, has long enjoyed a reputation for its colorful characters and eccentric personalities. In the nearly six decades that they lived there, Wilna Hervey and Nan Mason became two of the most famous and most beloved. With their impressive stature (Nan was almost as tall as Wilna), their openness as a same-sex couple, and their penchant for throwing the largest and wildest parties the town had ever seen, the "Big Girls," as they were affectionately known, became part of local legend.

Wilna and Nan playing golf. Shortly before leaving Hollywood for Woodstock in the spring of 1924, the girls play a round of golf. Both Wilna and Nan were very athletic and enjoyed a variety of sports, including horseback riding, swimming and softball.

As artists, Wilna and Nan explored every possible outlet for their creative talents during the years they lived in Woodstock, achieving recognition for a remarkable variety of art forms and genres. They surrounded themselves with notable artists and literary figures and numbered the most prominent among them as their closest friends. They also won the respect of the entire community for their tireless efforts to raise money for worthy causes and their willingness to help plan and organize civic events. Unfazed and unchanged by some of the challenges they faced and the extremes of wealth and poverty the passing years visited upon them, the two devoted companions became most famous of all for their steadfast determination to live life fully and for all it was worth. No one who encountered them—whether as entertainers, artists, farmers, clowns, volunteers, party planners—or simply as friends—ever forgot them.

This is their story.

CHAPTER 1

A Very Big Little Girl

No one thought it unusual that Wilna Hervey was such a large baby. But her rapid growth as a toddler signaled that something was amiss. Born in San Francisco on October 3rd, 1894, Wilna was the only child of William R. Hervey and Anna V. H. T. Hervey, although she had three half siblings by her mother's first marriage. Wilna's brother and two sisters were all of normal size and proportions. But Wilna was different. "By the time I was three, I was the size of a child of six," she recalled, "and twice as strong." And she kept growing. The child's size and strength—which she occasionally used to devastating effect—created challenges for Wilna's parents. Anna Hervey was compelled to prove her daughter's age so often that she took to carrying Wilna's birth certificate in her purse. Sending the child to school seemed inadvisable, as Wilna looked like a young adult at age six. Fearing that the youngster would be the victim of cruel taunting by the other children, and become a possible source of difficulty for the teachers due to her unusual strength, Wilna's mother decided to school her at home.[1]

Thus, young "Willie," as they called her, missed out on the experience of attending school with other children. In fact, she had no playmates at all as a child and would have no friends her own age until she was in her mid-teens. Hoping to compensate for their child's near total isolation and loneliness, her wealthy parents built an elaborate cocoon for their different daughter to grow up in. They lived in a mansion with servants, owned fine horses—which Wilna learned to ride—and kept a kennel of purebred dogs that became Wilna's surrogate playmates. The family went to museums and operas and traveled where and when they wished. Wilna had her own nurse, wonderful toys, dolls and clothes. She lacked for nothing—except a normal childhood. The formative experiences that children usually have interacting with other children, experiences that promote emotional growth and maturity, played no role in her upbringing. Part of Wilna's unique appeal to those who met her as an adult was her innocent demeanor and childlike outlook; both were the result of having lived in Neverland for the first fifteen years of her life.

Anna Van Horn Traphagen Hervey, c. 1895. This photo of Wilna's mother was kept, along with two of Wilna's baby pictures, in a small leather portfolio gold-embossed with the name William R. Hervey, Anna's husband and Wilna's doting father.

Wilna Hervey in 1895. Wilna was the only child of San Francisco music instructor William R. Hervey and his wealthy wife, Anna V. H. T. Hervey. By all accounts, little "Willie" was a very happy baby. She was also a very large baby, and that was only the beginning.

In retrospect, Wilna was grateful to have had "devoted parents who did everything in their power to give me a full happy childhood . . . and provide a cushion against the hurt of surprised stares and rude comments." But she also admitted that, as an adult, she went out into the world "shy, sensitive, and incredibly naïve."[2] In fact, thanks to a mother who not only sought to fulfill her every possible need but also made practical decisions for her, Wilna would all her life be a high-maintenance individual who was happiest in situations where others who loved her were able to do much the same.

There may have been a dark side to what Wilna once described as "the abnormal alchemy controlling my growth." Her conception, in the early years of her mother's second marriage, had taken Anna by surprise. The former Mrs. Thomas V. Cator already had three children between the ages of two and seven when she wedded William R. Hervey in 1892. She did not want another child, and in fact was so chagrined by her pregnancy that she attempted to induce a miscarriage. Exactly what she ingested, hoping to abort, is unknown. It didn't work, in any case, and Anna Hervey—who subsequently accepted and loved her daughter—apparently labored under the assumption that it was her fault that Wilna's growth hormones ran riot. A sense of guilt may have been mingled with her love for Wilna and intensified her need to constantly supervise her and to overprotect her.[3]

Wilna's parents were extremely well-to-do. Her mother, whose full maiden name was Anna Van Horn Traphagen Adams, came from a prominent New Jersey family whose pedigree included U.S. presidents and Civil War generals. The family's wealth was even more impressive than their ancestry, and Anna Hervey ended up being the sole heir of two maiden aunts of considerable means. In fact, the main reason for Wilna's family leaving San Francisco around 1900 and moving to Long Island, New York, was that her mother wanted to be near her recently inherited real estate holdings in New Jersey to better manage them. Not content to simply live off the proceeds of her properties, Anna Hervey—who identified herself as a "capitalist" in the 1915 New York state census—actively sought ways to maximize her income. In addition, Wilna's mother had not exactly walked away empty-handed from her first marriage, to a highly successful San Francisco lawyer and politician. Her second husband, William R. Hervey, while not nearly as wealthy, was nevertheless a professional man well paid for his efforts.[4]

William Hervey was a professional singer and voice coach who gave lessons from their home. He was not the only musician in the family, however. Wilna's mother was an accomplished pianist who occasionally performed in public. Wilna, like her half brother, Thomas Cator Jr., who was a composer, and her half sister Marie, who worked as a lyricist, received extensive training in music from childhood on. In a household where all cultural endeavors were appreciated, Wilna's interest in the visual arts began in her childhood with trips to art galleries and museums. Anna Hervey's home schooling of her daughter was a success: Wilna was well read and knowledgeable and had a sophisticated grasp of art and culture. She was also articulate in speech (albeit shy about expressing herself) and even as a youngster had a talent for expressing her thoughts in writing.

However, like so many young girls of the time, Wilna also developed a passion for movies and movie stars. Despite their distaste for such lowbrow entertainment, her parents tolerated this childish infatuation and permitted Wilna, once she reached her teens, to visit a small movie theater near their home in Far Rockaway, in the New York City borough of Queens. Little did Wilna dream, as a young teenager sitting spellbound in darkness, that she would one day appear on the screen herself and that the movies would be the vehicle by which she met the dearest friends of her life.

It was during a visit to the movies at age fifteen that Wilna acquired her first friend her own age. In those days of the silent cinema, every exhibitor provided live musical accompaniment for the films. While most big theaters had full orchestras, or special organs with built-in sound effects, the smallest houses often had to content themselves with just a piano. Wilna's local theater in Far Rockaway was one of the latter. One evening in 1910 Wilna found herself more impressed by the music than the movie it supported. After the show, she went down front to offer her compliments and discovered that the pianist was a diminutive fourteen-year-old girl named Muriel Pollock. Tiny, intense and a musical prodigy, "Molly" Pollock had already been playing in movie houses for several years. Wilna was so impressed that she invited the girl to come out to the family mansion on Oak Street to meet her musical family. She arranged for her father's chauffeur to pick Molly up.[5]

That one of the wealthiest and most socially prominent families in Far Rockaway would send their chauffeured limousine to fetch the daughter of an immigrant Russian Jew who ran a corner news stand was considered so remarkable that the story of this "untraditional" friendship was written up in the Brooklyn newspapers. William and Anna Hervey were as impressed with Molly as Wilna had expected and Molly became a frequent visitor to their home. The Herveys were not only stunned by Molly's musical abilities but also impressed by her seriousness and common sense. For all practical purposes, Molly was a tiny adult. Her parents had fallen on very hard times a few years before. When they reached the point of desperation, Molly had gone out and found a job playing for movies. She had been doing it ever since.[6]

Wilna and Molly quickly became inseparable. While it may have seemed on the surface that two girls from such different backgrounds could have little in common, they each found in the other someone who understood an important aspect of their existence. They were both "outsiders," Wilna because of her size—she had now reached six-foot-three and weighed over three hundred pounds—and Molly because she had functioned as an adult since the age of twelve. Neither of them had experienced a normal childhood, and neither had the typical social life of a teenaged girl. They made a comical team. Molly was so short that she could stand under Wilna's outstretched arm. Yet she was the "boss," with a temperament that bordered on the dictatorial at times, and she frequently scolded Wilna when her cluelessness or casual attention to important details became too much to bear.[7] With Molly's help and guidance, Wilna would timidly venture out into the world beyond her family's protective borders. The two would remain close friends until Molly's death more than sixty years later.

CHAPTER 2

"Wilna Wilde"

Opposite: Wilna Hervey, Self-Portrait. *This charcoal sketch was done during Wilna's first year at Adelphi College, Brooklyn, in 1914 when she was twenty. It is the earliest known example of her art work.*

Because of their own musical accomplishments, both of Wilna's parents hoped their daughter might pursue a musical career. But Wilna had other ideas. As she facetiously told a reporter in 1930, "There were three concert grands going at all times. You could hardly hear yourself talk. Musical as I was, I hadn't the heart to add to the din—and so I decided to be a painter."[1] In fact, Wilna took an interest in the visual arts in early childhood and her parents allowed her to pursue her passion. At age twelve, Wilna was provided with painting lessons at the studio of Alexandrina Robertson Harris in Brooklyn. Mrs. Harris, a miniaturist best known today for her tiny portrait of Amelia Earhart in the collection of the Smithsonian American Art Museum, was only twenty-two years old and just beginning her career. Not only did she have a considerable impact on the shy young girl who towered above her, inspiring an interest in portraiture as well as miniatures, she and Wilna quickly bonded and became friends for life.

It was Alexandrina Harris who guided Wilna to the next phase of her education, taking her timid teenaged pupil, who thus far had never sat in a classroom with other children, to her alma mater, Adelphi College in Brooklyn, for a personal introduction. At Adelphi, Wilna met Harris's own mentor, the distinguished artist John B. Whittaker. With his full gray beard and gentle demeanor, he reminded Wilna of the poet Longfellow and she took an instant liking to him. Sensitive to her insecurities and charmed by her naïve demeanor, Whittaker took the big little girl under his wing and made sure she felt quite secure as she enrolled in a program of study that included academic subjects as well as art. Wilna's earliest surviving art works—a group of six charcoal sketches—date from her years at Adelphi. Aside from an anatomical study of a muscular male arm, all the pieces are portrait studies, including a pensive self-portrait, an indication that Wilna's desire to be a portrait artist was present in the earliest stages of her training. Significantly, the Adelphi College yearbooks for the years that Wilna attended make virtually no mention of her. Not yet ready or able to come out of her shell, Wilna did not participate in any of the clubs, plays or social activities enjoyed by the other girls.[2]

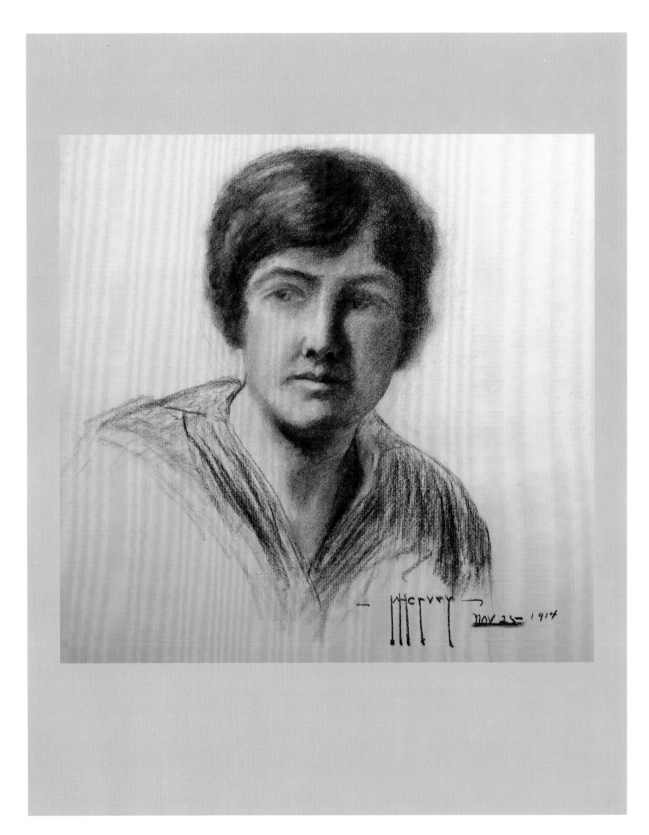

Adelphi College Art Department, c. 1914. Wilna's professor, John B. Whittaker, is at right. Wilna wrote to a friend: "This is your Willie's art class with our dear old teacher—I just love him . . . I spend such happy hours here trying so hard to draw."[1]

Much to her parents' chagrin, Wilna's intensive art training and college studies did not diminish her passion for the movies. On the contrary, it continued to grow. Like so many young women of the day, she read the latest fan magazines each month and fantasized about meeting the stars or even being in a movie herself. Unlike most other young women, however, Wilna had the means to live out her fantasies. Her older half sister, Eleanor Cator, was engaged to Eugene V. Brewster, the editor of *Motion Picture Magazine*. Brewster had many friends in the movie business and important connections to several movie studios.[3] Brewster was more than glad to score a few points with his fiancée by opening doors for her baby sister, and the young film fan was more than happy to dash through them. He not only published two short articles by Wilna in his magazine but also helped her get her first small part in a motion picture. As Wilna's parents thought of the flickers as one of the more unpleasant aspects of modern life, they were certain to be dyspeptic when they discovered that their cultured daughter had ventured outside the realm of high art to slum it in movieland. Therefore, Wilna made her first screen appearance under the name "Wilna Wilde," and conveniently forgot to tell them about it.[4]

Wilna's generous size made her a natural for silent comedy sight gags, and it was as a possible comic figure that she was introduced to the popular comedy team of Mr. and Mrs. Sidney Drew in 1916. She made her first screen appearance in their one-reel film *Help!* that same year. As a hopeful in an employment office, Wilna walks through

Above: Wilna Hervey, Unidentified Woman. *One of a series of portraits Wilna created in her drawing classes at Adelphi College, this charcoal drawing from 1915 shows a marked improvement when compared to her self-portrait sketched only five months earlier.*

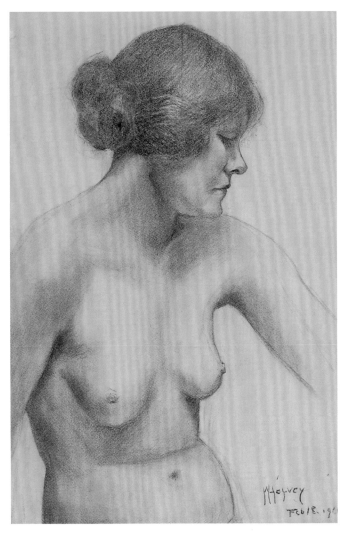

Left: Wilna Hervey, Nude Figure Study. *Another in the series of portraits Wilna sketched while attending Adelphi College, this 1916 figure demonstrates her steadily improving skills as a draftswoman. Wilna's interest in realistic portraiture developed early in her training.*

the room making a rude face at the Drews, who have got the job she was after. She is onscreen for less than twenty seconds and is not fully visible the whole time. In a somewhat larger role, Wilna portrayed a cook in another of the Drews' domestic comedies in 1917. An item published in *Motion Picture Classic Magazine* in 1917 claimed that Sidney Drew personally discovered Wilna as she frolicked on the beach at Far Rockaway, but that was a contrived bit of fluff—it was more interesting than the fact that the magazine's editor had assisted Drew in his "discovery." As only a handful of the Drew comedies survive today, we have no way of knowing how many of the films Wilna appeared in or how meaningful her parts might have been. A couple of years later she would also appear in three comedies made by the vaudeville star Johnny Dooley. The details are sparse here as well, and the films do not survive.[5]

Wilna discovered something important through her first movie roles. While it had always hurt her to find that people were staring at her and giggling when she walked down the street or into a restaurant, the circumstances felt quite different when she took control of the situation and purposely used her size to provoke amazement and laughter in a comic scene. Using her ample proportions as an actress meant that the reactions she got were a benchmark of success. This was something to be enjoyed rather than feared. Wilna learned something else from her first fleeting appearances before the camera: movie work paid extremely well. Even these initial minor roles paid her more in one day than many factory workers collected after a week of hard work. With this discretionary cash—which she also neglected to tell her parents about right away—she bought her first car, a secondhand Dort that she kept hidden in Manhattan for several months.

Now in her twenties, cautiously emerging from her cocoon and craving more personal space apart from her loving but suffocating parents, Wilna came to the realization that a healthy income from making movies might provide her with the financial independence that would be the best route to that goal. Therefore, even though she intended to make art her primary passion and pursuit, Wilna got herself an agent in hopes of finding more lucrative work in the movies.

Right: Wilna with silent comedy star Sidney Drew. In this unidentified 1917 film Wilna (credited as Wilna Wilde) played a cook hired by Drew and his wife. The original publicity tag accompanying the photo read: "'She's simply got to make good,' says Sid. 'If she doesn't, who's going to discharge her? Not me!'"[2]

CHAPTER 3

Greenwich Village and Woodstock

The high regard held by Wilna's parents for Molly Pollock's sound judgment proved to be of great benefit to Wilna in 1916, when Molly took a job with a music publisher and moved to a small, one-room, apartment in Manhattan. Wilna, now nearly twenty-two years old, longed to follow her best friend's lead and enjoy her own taste of freedom. Her parents—her mother in particular—would countenance no such notion. However, in 1917, when Wilna enrolled in drawing classes at the Winold Reiss studio school in Greenwich Village, she saw an opportunity. Classes ran until ten at night and that meant a very late journey home on the Long Island Railroad. Wilna suggested to her parents that it might be more practical for her to stay in the city a few nights a week, *with Molly*. Reluctantly—and only because of Molly—they finally agreed.

Considering her early interest in portraiture, Wilna's decision to study with a dynamic figure like Winold Reiss was fortuitous. The German-born Reiss was already well known in the Manhattan art community in 1917, thanks to his interior designs, his lectures at the Art Students League, his newly founded magazine, *Modern Art Collector*, and the art school he had established in 1915. His considerable skill as a portrait artist was already in evidence and rapidly growing; he would emerge as one of the most significant portrait artists of the twentieth century.

Reiss had only recently moved his studio and school to the location where Wilna went to take her drawing lessons—Four Christopher Street. There he gave classes from nine in the morning until two in the afternoon, followed by an extended break. Classes resumed from seven to ten in the evening. Wilna took advantage of the five-hour interval to sketch, shop or visit Manhattan museums. Following this daily schedule, retiring to Molly's tiny first-floor flat at the end of the day, and not having to go back home to her parents, was sheer bliss.[1]

Winold Reiss had a generous professional nature, a warm, pleasant demeanor and an open personality, in addition to his intellect and considerable talent. Students loved

Left: Wilna at the Winold Reiss studio. In this view of the Christopher Street studio in Manhattan, Wilna's teacher, mentor and friend Winold Reiss looks over her shoulder as she sketches. The young woman at Wilna's left is Andrée Ruellan, who would ultimately become one of her closest friends in Woodstock.

Right: Drawing class at the Winold Reiss studio. It is noteworthy that in both of these photos of the Christopher Street studio, Reiss is seen watching Wilna as she works. Early in Wilna's training, Reiss recognized her talent. His suggestion that she attend the summer school of painting at Woodstock had far-reaching consequences.

him, and Wilna was no exception. After hours of lessons, sketching, critiquing and more lessons, Reiss encouraged everyone to relax and refresh themselves with singing, games and other recreational activities. Sometimes they cranked up a Victrola that Reiss kept in the studio and danced. On occasion, Reiss invited a recently arrived Austrian friend to come by and play spirited dance music on his violin. The fiddler's name was Fritz Kreisler.

"In that informal atmosphere and in the company of people with kindred interests, a great deal of my shyness evaporated," Wilna recalled.[2] As an adult, Wilna was finding it easier to make friends and started making up for all those years of being a lonely child. Her wide-eyed air of innocent vulnerability and childlike enthusiasm for anything new, contrasted with her astonishing size, endeared her to many of her new acquaintances, as did the sincere personal interest and generosity she showed toward strangers. At the Reiss studio, she no longer felt awkward for being different. Small wonder. There was a lot of "different" going on at Four Christopher Street.

There was a nightclub in the basement of the building, and one of the storefronts on the first floor—when it wasn't being rented—was occupied by a Zulu dancer named Congo, who sometimes forgot to close the curtains over the show windows when he was setting fire to his hair (as opposed to cutting it) or rehearsing dance routines with the pet boa constrictor he kept under his bed. The protean vaudeville entertainer Sylvester "Bubi" Schaeffer, whose act included magic, feats of strength, juggling, trick shooting, violin playing and painting, was often in attendance, as were figures of the Harlem Renaissance, the still-notorious Evelyn Nesbit, and assorted dancers and poets. With nude models always on display, the local mounted police officer popped in frequently, hoping to get an eyeful.[3] There were good reasons why the stories Wilna told her mother each weekend were carefully edited.

It was because of Winold Reiss that Wilna made her first trip to Woodstock, New York, and fell in love with the valley in the Catskills that would become her home for nearly

The village of Woodstock, New York, as it looked when Wilna visited for the first time in 1918. It was already gaining a reputation as one of the pre-eminent artist colonies in the country. By the end of her first summer there, Wilna had fallen in love with the spirited bohemian atmosphere of this quaint hamlet in the Catskills.

sixty years. In the summers of 1916 and 1917, Reiss moved his art school to Woodstock for the season and was well acquainted with the art colony developing there. Already impressed by Wilna's talent and devotion to her training, Reiss suggested she attend the 1918 summer school of painting being offered in Woodstock by the Art Students League.

Wilna's parents agreed to let her spend the summer away from home largely because she would have adult supervision, in the form of Molly. Having already published several songs, Molly wanted to get away somewhere to work on more compositions and agreed that a summer in Woodstock was a great idea. After keeping her car hidden in the city for months, Wilna suddenly unveiled it for her flummoxed parents just before heading off to the Catskills. In April 1918 the two friends tied a mattress on the roof of the Dort, loaded the car with enough clothes and supplies to last the summer, and rumbled off to Woodstock.[4]

Though today it presents the welcome aspect of a village nestled in the woods, Woodstock in 1918 had a very different appearance. The main thoroughfare and its connecting side streets and country lanes stretched across a much more open countryside. Thanks to extensive deforestation in the previous century, the vast hemlock forests that once blanketed the area were gone, leaving only sparse second growth in those few areas where there were any trees at all. Efforts to expand farmland had kept large areas of countryside open, even far up the sides of the mountains that dominated the landscape. Most of Woodstock's streets were as yet unpaved, electrification was a few years away and much of the plumbing was still outdoors. A few telephones had been installed but service was limited.

Prior to the coming of the artists, Woodstock had been a sleepy farming community that retained its nineteenth-century appearance. It had no industry and was largely populated by old-fashioned folks of modest means. But the artists *had* come, starting in 1902 with the arrival of the wealthy Englishman Ralph Whitehead with his colleagues

Bolton Brown and Hervey White. The three men established the Arts and Crafts colony Byrdcliffe on the slopes of Mount Guardian overlooking the village, building homes, a library, and shops for furniture-making, pottery, painting, metal work and weaving.

In 1904 Hervey White, tiring of Whitehead's dictatorial management style, came down from the mountain and bought a large farm in West Hurley, just southeast of the village of Woodstock. There, on his one-hundred-and-two-acre spread, he built his Maverick Art Colony as a kind of socialistic counterpoint to the elitism of Byrdcliffe. An eccentric social activist and idealist, Hervey White welcomed writers, musicians, craftsmen, actors and artists to join him in living there in a series of rustic cabins that he made available, more often than not rent free. White also encouraged everyone to join him in casting off society's restrictions. "Do what you want to (as long as you don't harm others)," was his simple guiding principle. His influence on the growth of Woodstock as an art colony and a haven for free thinkers and free spirits cannot be overstated.

Finally, in 1906, attracted by both Byrdcliffe and the Maverick, the Manhattan-based Art Students League moved its summer school of painting from Old Lyme, Connecticut, to Woodstock, taking over an old livery stable and undertaker's shop in the center of town. Over the years a remarkable mix of creative talents migrated to Woodstock and combined with some of the more quirky local characters to create a unique, comfortable and tolerant haven for even the most eccentric artistic personalities. While the local residents were not always happy with the migration of bohemian youngsters to their community from Greenwich Village, or with the tourists who sometimes arrived just to gawk at the flamboyant behavior and dress of the *artistes*, they came in time to appreciate the economic benefits of this transformation of their town.

When Wilna and Molly set foot in this rare and wonderful artistic world in the summer of 1918, the first thing they discovered was that it was crowded. With artists of one sort or another expanding the population of Woodstock by up to twenty-five percent each summer, finding a place to stay proved problematic. It was out of necessity that many of the young pilgrims flocking there contented themselves with living in shacks and bathing in streams. With some difficulty, the two friends managed to rent the loft of a barn at an economical twelve dollars for the summer. When they finished sweeping out the straw and setting mousetraps—the latter a ritual that would need repeating every day—they went out in search of a piano for Molly. With the help of a few young men Wilna knew from her studies in Manhattan, they managed to find an old upright and wrestle it up the rickety steps to the loft.[5]

"That was a wonderful summer," Wilna remembered. "We worked hard all day, Mollie [sic] at composing and I at painting. We met several artists and musicians and actors and writers who were later to become famous and make the name of Woodstock well known."[6] Among the artists with whom Wilna studied that summer was Henry Lee McFee, who would have a significant impact on Wilna's artistic development and become one of her many Woodstock friends. She made the acquaintance of two other artists that summer. Charles Rosen, spending his first season there as a teacher and soon to return as a permanent resident, and Eugene Speicher, who had been living in the community for several years, would also become Wilna's close friends.

Wilna Hervey painting at Woodstock. The summer school of painting organized by the Art Students League at Woodstock focused on landscape painting in the open air. This tiny snapshot shows Wilna working to capture the mountain scenery in the summer of 1918.

Quickly realizing that Woodstock harbored more unique personalities and free spirits than the Reiss studio in Manhattan, Wilna immediately felt at home and reveled in the freedom she felt there. It did not take long for her and Molly to plunge into the spirit of Woodstock. Molly took time out from her work to stage a musical benefit for the Red Cross, and Wilna participated in the biggest community event of the summer, the fourth Maverick Festival, which arrived with the August full moon. The zany costumed celebration of life in song, dance, food and high spirits had been inaugurated in 1915 by Hervey White to raise cash for drilling a well. Because of the First World War, an absurd pageant lampooning the Kaiser was staged in 1918 and Wilna was drafted for service to lead the "Russian women's battalion of death" into the onstage melee.[7] By the end of her first summer in Woodstock, Wilna had fallen in love with the town, the countryside and the congenial atmosphere of the art colony. This was where she wanted to settle down, she decided. Her dream of buying land and building a home there would come true only a few years later.

Returning to Manhattan in the fall, Wilna resumed her instruction at the Winold Reiss studio. She would continue to enroll there for the next two years, alternating with additional lessons in Woodstock each summer. By 1919 Wilna had developed several close friendships at the Reiss studio. Chief among these friends was Reiss himself, who was increasingly impressed by Wilna's artistic potential. With his wife, Henriette, Reiss began to invite Wilna to social gatherings in their quarters on the upper floors of the studio building. Reiss's keen interest in observing and rendering honest images of ethnic types had a profound influence on Wilna, which can be seen in portraits she drew and painted as late as 1940. In addition to her growing friendship with Reiss, Wilna cultivated a warm regard for Reiss's friend and fellow German émigré Bubi Schaeffer and for Reiss's prize pupil, W. Langdon "Billy" Kihn.[8]

The studio on Christopher Street was also the source of Wilna's first serious romance. One evening in 1919, as the students were unwinding after a long day of lessons, Wilna

Eva Watson-Schütze, Wilna Hervey, Woodstock. The earliest known instance of Wilna posing for an artist, this serene and pensive image likely dates from 1918, Wilna's first season in Woodstock. Her elegant attire suggests the wealth she came from, a factor that set her apart from the average art student in Woodstock in those years.

overheard one of the men bragging about his great strength. With everyone in a silly mood (they had just been playing leapfrog), she yelled out a humorous challenge: "I bet there isn't one man here who can pick me up!" Whereupon a young man she had seen around the studio a couple of times ran over and quite literally swept Wilna off her feet. He not only picked her up as though she weighed no more than a girl one third her size, but carried her all around the big studio before setting her down to cheers, laughter and applause. His name was Karoly Fulop, and before he left his native Hungary to study art in America he had been a circus strongman and acrobat. Wilna was impressed by this tall, handsome and extremely strong stranger with a charming accent. For his part, Karoly was equally impressed by the buxom young Valkyrie he had just gathered into his arms. For the next several weeks they were inseparable, with the ambitious acrobat/artist making several pilgrimages to the Hervey mansion in Far Rockaway.[9]

Karoly was extremely talented and would in time evolve into a successful sculptor, painter, and watercolorist with a remarkable and distinctive style. In 1919, however, he was still finding his way, taking lessons from Reiss and working on a variety of experimental projects in his own studio. Convinced that he was prostituting his talent by working as a commercial artist, he had just given up a lucrative job to devote his full energies to his quest for pure art. The fact that he had nothing to live on seemed not to concern him. What Karoly lacked in material success, he more than made up for in strong opinions about art, women and life in general. Totally smitten with Wilna, he urged her to abandon her parents and come live with him in his bleak garret. He was quite annoyed when she refused. Karoly bristled at any mention of Wilna's bit parts in films and insisted that this was something she should never consider doing again. Her expressed desires to achieve personal independence, travel and buy property in Woodstock were all rejected as ambitions that could only serve to take his beloved away from him. This tempestuous relationship, with its cycle of "poetic ecstasy or tragic depression," as Wilna described it, would continue, on and off, for years, punctuated by several separations—each one "forever"—and fervent promises that neither would ever marry anyone else.[10]

In the summer of 1919, as Winold Reiss began planning his first trip west to study and paint the Blackfoot Indians in Montana, he asked his two best students— Billy Kihn and Wilna Hervey—to accompany him. The trip was scheduled for the following January. Wilna was delighted at the prospect, but her excitement was short-lived. "What would people think if you went off to Montana with two men?" her mother asked. Wilna would later see the hand of destiny at work in Anna Hervey's emphatic rejection of the wonderful opportunity that Reiss had laid before her. Had she gone to Montana, she never would have made the movies for which she became famous. For it was not long after her mother torpedoed the trip to Montana that Wilna was summoned to her agent's office in Manhattan. He thought she might be perfect for a really big part.[11]

The artist Karoly Fulop. This rare photo of Wilna's ardent suitor shows the Hungarian strongman-turned-artist as he would have appeared in 1920 when he literally swept Wilna off her feet at the Winold Reiss studio. His air of self-confidence is palpable, and his hair seems as unruly as his temperament.

CHAPTER 4

"The Original Katrinka"

Wilna Hervey would long remember the interview in New York that changed her life. She arrived at her agent's office to find him engaged in conversation with another man, who was impatiently pacing up and down. As Wilna entered the room, the pacing stopped and the man looked up. "My God!" he exclaimed. "She is the original Katrinka!"[1] Expressing his astonishment—and delight—was the noted cartoonist Fontaine Fox, creator of the Toonerville Trolley cartoons, which were then syndicated in several hundred newspapers around the country. Milking his success for all it was worth, Fox had taken to franchising his Toonerville brand in every imaginable way. There would soon be Toonerville games, Toonerville windup toys, and even Toonerville salt and pepper shakers. At the request of the Betzwood Film Company, operating out of a studio in the Philadelphia suburbs, he had also recently agreed to produce a series of two-reel live action comedies with actors taking the roles of his beloved Toonerville Folks. Fox planned to write the scenarios himself and had come to New York with the studio's general manager to search for actors and actresses to star in his comedies.

One of the most popular of Fox's inventions was the character of Powerful Katrinka, a massive young woman of superhuman strength, and limited mental range, who was capable of lifting the trolley off the tracks. She occasionally carried a loaded wheelbarrow in front of her because she hadn't thought to put the wheel down on the ground. Properly casting this role was essential to the success of the proposed Toonerville films. The actress needed to be enormous and very strong, as not all of the feats of strength would be sight gags. She also needed to have an air of oblivious innocence. Not surprisingly, Wilna got the part.

With the Betzwood Film Company already gearing up for production, it was necessary for Wilna to leave almost immediately for the sprawling studio twenty miles northwest of Philadelphia. She spent several days alternating between frenzied packing and equally frenzied attempts to override her parents' objections to her leaving home.

Left: The Betzwood motion picture studio in the Philadelphia suburbs. The three large structures are the stages where interior shots for Wilna's Toonerville movies were filmed. The small buildings in the foreground are film storage vaults. Wilna spent two summers here in the role of "The Powerful Katrinka" opposite Dan Mason.

Right: Trying to balance the trolley. Maintaining equilibrium was not easy when Katrinka stepped off the Toonerville Trolley. When cartoonist Fontaine Fox designed the trolley car to be used by the Betzwood Film Company, he balanced it precariously on one set of wheels to allow for cinematic moments like this.

Cast and crew of the Toonerville Trolley comedies. On location during the filming of the first of the Toonerville Trolley movies, the entire cast and crew posed for a studio publicity shot. Director Robert Eddy stands on the trolley platform beside Dan Mason. Wilna considered Bob Eddy to be the best director she ever worked with.

Moving the Toonerville Trolley off the tracks. Since the Toonerville films were made on an active trolley line near the Betzwood studio, movie-making occasionally prevented the real trolley from making its scheduled run. On those occasions the Toonerville Trolley had to be wrestled off the tracks and then put back once the line was clear.

Having missed out on a trip to Montana with Winold Reiss, Wilna insisted she would not be denied the opportunity to have a starring role in a motion picture. Wilna had been promised one hundred and fifty dollars a week—about five times what the average skilled factory worker was making in those days. Using this hefty salary as leverage, she ultimately won her parents' grudging acceptance of her plans. The tradeoff was an agreement that she would return home to the safety of the family nest every weekend. And, to spare the family eternal disgrace and scandal, she would continue to be credited as Wilna Wilde.

In October 1919, instead of basking in the convivial atmosphere of the Winold Reiss studio in Greenwich Village, Wilna Hervey found herself living in a small, sparsely furnished room in a seedy family-run hotel in Norristown, Pennsylvania. The Hartranft House was only a short train ride from the Betzwood studio, where she was about to take on a significant movie role. She was completely on her own for the first time in her life, the independence she sought guaranteed by a sizeable weekly salary. But there was no mother or Molly to talk to or help her organize her thoughts. She felt very isolated.[2]

Fortunately, her loneliness didn't last long. During her first days at the studio, Wilna noticed that a small, quiet, bearded man watched her intently as she went through a series of screen tests. His name was Dan Mason and he had been hired to portray

The Powerful Katrinka boards the Toonerville Trolley. The Skipper (Dan Mason) watches nervously as Katrinka approaches carrying a steamer trunk as her "purse." On the left, seated in front of the camera, is director Robert Eddy.

Katrinka rides with the freight. In this small snapshot from Wilna's personal album, Katrinka can be seen riding on a flatbed car behind the Toonerville Trolley. Sight gags occasionally showed Wilna hoisting this car on and off the tracks with her bare hands.

the most important of all the Toonerville Folks, the eccentric and irascible "Skipper," who pilots the derelict trolley. When the studio's general manager, Ira Lowry, introduced them, Mason warmly embraced the inexperienced young actress and began providing her with much needed personal attention and kindly advice. "If I had any doubts about my choice of work before, Dan allayed them," Wilna remembered. "He became mentor, coach, and very dear friend."[3]

Dan Mason, whose real name was Daniel L. Grassman, was a veteran entertainer with fifty years' experience in vaudeville, theater and the movies before coming to the Betzwood studio. The son of German immigrants, he got his start on the stage as a dialect comedian. From vaudeville Dan had moved into musical comedy. He was the original "Prince of Pilsen" and had appeared in numerous touring productions of such popular pieces as *Peck's Bad Boy*. At one point he even headed up his own successful company, Dan Mason Comedies. The programs he devised featured his wife, Millicent Page, an entertainer he had met and married while on tour in 1886.[4]

Around 1910, when Dan was in his late fifties, he decided to explore the possibilities offered by the burgeoning movie industry. It was the start of a second career. In 1913 he secured a position with the Edison Motion Picture Company as an actor and scenario writer. From there he went on to work for several other film production companies, establishing a reputation as a fine character actor appearing opposite Theda Bara, Will

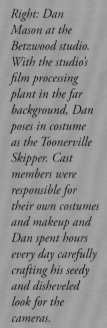

Right: Dan Mason at the Betzwood studio. With the studio's film processing plant in the far background, Dan poses in costume as the Toonerville Skipper. Cast members were responsible for their own costumes and makeup and Dan spent hours every day carefully crafting his seedy and disheveled look for the cameras.

Above: The actor Dan Mason as himself. Signed "to Wilna Hervey," this rare photograph shows Wilna's comedy co-star out of makeup and costume, holding a publicity shot of himself portraying one of his many movie personas. Dan's face was a blank canvas that he skillfully transformed into hundreds of unique characters during his fifty years in show business.

Rogers and John Barrymore.[5] Casting Dan Mason as the Toonerville Skipper was the most inspired choice made by Fontaine Fox and the Betzwood Film Company producers and was pivotal to the success of the Toonerville Trolley films.

Dan Mason was also living at the Hartranft House and began knocking on Wilna's door every morning, eating breakfast with her and riding with her on the train to the studio. He taught her how to apply greasepaint—which Wilna had never even heard of—and showed her how to avoid hurting herself when the scenarios called for her to

Right: "I've been layin' for that hen." After the Skipper runs over a chicken that was roosting on the trolley tracks, Katrinka helps him prepare the fresh poultry for sale.

Left: "She was a Swede who raised Poles." No, it's not a real telephone pole, but the role of Katrinka was physically grueling and required real strength and stamina on Wilna's part. The outrageous puns that accompanied both of these publicity photos were prime examples of the Toonerville films' folksy humor.

take heavy falls. She learned how to time entrances and exits. With Dan's help, Wilna needed fewer retakes and her self-confidence began to soar. Wilna soon learned that while imbued with a genuinely kind nature, Dan had another reason for so quickly befriending her: he was as lonely as she was. Millicent Page, his wife of thirty-three years, had died only a few months earlier, just before he was offered the role of Skipper.[6] The friendship of Dan Mason and Wilna Hervey contributed much to their onscreen chemistry, and the Toonerville Trolley films were the better for it.

Powerful Katrinka meets the tilting tea table. Unable to figure out the mind-numbing complexities of a table with a top that folds down, Katrinka ends up using it as a serving tray instead.

The cast members of the Toonerville comedies were responsible for assembling their own costumes. For the first time ever, Wilna enjoyed putting together an ensemble designed to showcase her generous proportions. Raiding the Salvation Army thrift store near her hotel, she wrapped herself in a long skirt with a checkered blouse, found a jacket that didn't quite fit, and bought shoes so awful that she would receive fan mail from halfway round the world sympathizing with her for having to wear them. As a finishing touch, she pulled her hair up onto her head—giving her several more inches of height—and topped it with an absurdly tiny hat.

Dan Mason dressed to look as seedy and unkempt as possible. His clothes were rumpled, and while one pant leg was always tucked in his boot, the other always hung out. Normally bald and clean-shaven, Dan carefully applied wisps of grey hair and a full beard, strand by strand, on a daily basis to craft the visage of the wizened old Skipper. By stooping slightly to enhance the impression of age, the five-foot-four-inch actor also emphasized the difference between his height and Wilna's, making their encounters all the more comical. His mannerisms and facial expressions won him rave reviews.

In addition to Wilna Hervey and Dan Mason, there was a third "star" of the Toonerville films—the trolley itself. At the Betzwood studio, Fontaine Fox designed and built a full-scale version of his dilapidated cartoon trolley. It sat precariously balanced on one set of wheels so that it was easily tipped front to back when someone heavy—like Katrinka—tried to board. Though it lacked a motor of any kind, the studio found ingenious methods for creating the illusion of the trolley's motion, pushing and pulling the contraption in a variety of ways that the camera never saw.

Most of the exterior work on the Toonerville comedies was done in the tiny hamlet of Williams Corner, just outside the town of Phoenixville, some seven miles west of the Betzwood studio. In the middle of this quaint community of antique frame buildings and a covered bridge sat the trolley-car barn used by the Phoenixville, Valley Forge & Strafford Railway, a nearly defunct single-track transportation company serving that rural part of Chester County, Pennsylvania. The Betzwood Film Company arranged to keep the Toonerville Trolley in the PVF&S car barn at night, and every morning rolled it out onto the tracks to shoot its scenes. Wilna remembered that on several occasions, when production was running behind schedule and the real trolley was sitting on the tracks with an impatient conductor waiting to get by, the studio crew had to round up half a dozen husky men, lift the Toonerville Trolley off the tracks and move it aside. Then they had to put it back again to resume filming.[7]

Wilna's portrayal of Katrinka was set in the context of an ongoing series of sight gags intended to play up the notion of Katrinka's superhuman strength and clueless innocence. In the pilot film for the series, *The Toonerville Trolley That Meets All Trains*, Katrinka disrupts the trolley line and derails an impending wedding when she sees a snake and rips up a section of the trolley tracks to defend herself against the varmint. In *The Skipper's Narrow Escape*, she attempts to kill a mouse with a baseball bat, only to ruin the plumbing, which she is then obliged to fix by twisting the pipes with her bare hands. She lifts up a ladder to give the person standing on it a better view in *The Skipper's Flirtation*, and carries off her employer, the Terrible Tempered Mr. Bangs, like a sack of flour when the moonshine proves a bit too much in *The Skipper's 'Boozem' Friends*. Katrinka totes heavy furniture, brings in the laundry—clotheslines, poles and all—lifts the trolley to retrieve a dead chicken, tosses telephone poles about and generally performs all needed heavy tasks, breaking everything but a sweat.

Powerful Katrinka brings in the laundry. Super-strong and utterly clueless, Katrinka has an unfortunate habit of taking simple instructions much too literally.

CHAPTER 5

Dan Mason's Daughter

Dan Mason frequently mentioned to Wilna how much he missed his daughter, Nan, and worried about her living alone in their rented house back in New York. The fact that she had a fiancé, and was home alone, especially worried him for fear "the neighbors might talk." He also hated living in a hotel. Frugal old German that he was, Dan resented paying for a room and having nothing to show for it while renting a home in the Bronx that he wasn't living in. The solution to all of these problems, he decided, was for him to buy a house near the studio and for Nan to come down to Pennsylvania and keep him company. As her fiancé, Arthur Ryan, was leaving New York to live with his family in Florida until their wedding the following March, Nan agreed to her father's plan. She quit her job as a stenographer and scheduled her arrival in Norristown for a weekend in April 1920.

Wilna was both excited and apprehensive about meeting Dan's daughter. Missing her mother and Molly, she looked forward to the possibility of having a female friend close at hand to confide in. But she worried that Nan Mason might not like her. Because of Dan's age, Wilna pictured his daughter as a quiet older woman, matronly perhaps, and assumed that Dan's small stature meant that Nan would be rather small herself. The big-boned, boisterous and very young woman who showed up took her completely by surprise.

On the appointed day, Dan and Wilna were relaxing in the lobby of the hotel waiting until it was time to walk down to the station and meet Nan's train. Dan was smoking a cigar and chatting with other guests while Wilna sat in an alcove writing letters. Suddenly a brassy voice rang through the lobby: "Where's my Dad?" It was Nan. She had taken an earlier train and, unable to alert them, had walked up from the station singlehandedly dragging all her luggage and toting her pet tomcat in a cage.[1] Stunned by the sight of this tall, "healthy, strong, rosey-cheeked" young woman, Wilna timidly emerged from her alcove to say hello. Neither girl was quite sure what to say or do, astonished as they were by their first impressions of each other. Though she certainly had been advised of Wilna's size, it took Nan a moment to process meeting the real thing. She

Nan Mason, Atlantic City, 1915. The earliest known image of Nan Mason, this photo was taken on the Boardwalk in Atlantic City the year she turned nineteen. Her meeting with Wilna Hervey was still five years into the future.

later recalled that, as she entered the hotel lobby, she had seen a face peering around the curtain of the alcove looking at her, then watched in amazement as the face slowly rose higher and higher in the doorway, as Wilna stood up from her chair. "For Dan's sake, we were both prepared to like each other," Wilna recalled. "For Dan's sake we each hid our mutual dismay."[2]

The following week, Nan accompanied her father and Wilna to the studio to watch the movie-making in progress. The daily routine provided the two young women time to talk on the train, during breaks and in the evening back at the hotel. Both cautiously probed for areas of common interest and experience. Nan later admitted that these early conversations left her feeling inferior. If Wilna mentioned riding her father's fine horses, Nan was reluctant to admit that her experience with horses was limited to being placed on a pony to have her picture taken as a child. Wilna's education, thanks to her mother and the quality of instruction at Adelphi College, had given her the facility to talk knowledgably on a wide range of topics, and her years of art training weighed heavily against Nan's admission that she "used to sketch a little" when she was in school. And, although Nan was quite talented musically, the piano lessons she had taken seemed feeble competition for the musical prowess of the entire Cator/Hervey family.[3]

Compared to Wilna, who had enjoyed a very secure and sheltered childhood, living in one house in one community most of her life, Nan had lived an unsettled youth due to the peripatetic nature of her parents' profession. Even after the Mason family stopped touring, they still moved from place to place, leaving Manhattan for Atlantic City, then Atlantic City for the Bronx. Nan's childhood may have been unsettled emotionally as well. Although her father doted on her as his only daughter, and Nan was extremely close to her mother, the family was often torn apart by turmoil caused by her older brother, Harry. Dan and Millicent Mason had lost two young sons while touring in vaudeville in the years before Nan's birth. Their only surviving son, Harry, was a troubled man whose flair for dysfunction caused his parents no end of grief and anxiety. Exactly what Harry's issues were is not known, but reading between the lines of Dan Mason's surviving letters, one can see that he blamed his son's behavior for Millicent's untimely death in 1919.[4]

It was Nan Mason's saving grace that she was by nature a relentlessly cheerful individual with a knack for making the best of difficult situations. Prone to bear hugs and effusive expression of her sentiments, she was accommodating and not easily upset. It was typical of Nan's approach to life that, as she pondered her future, she took practical measures to become self-sufficient in a dependable and predictable career. Upon graduation from high school, Nan had enrolled in a small business college and trained as a stenographer. She then took a job with the Liverpool and London and Globe Insurance Company in Manhattan, commuting from the family home in the Bronx. A boyfriend named Arthur Ryan and a proposal of marriage followed. By 1920, Nan Mason thought she had her whole future figured out; she would be a very conventional wife, mother and homemaker. In fact, none of that was destined to come true.

Shortly after Nan arrived, Dan Mason bought a small Craftsman-style bungalow in the hamlet of Audubon, just two and a half miles northwest of the Betzwood studio. Like

Williams Corner, where the Toonerville films were being shot, Audubon was one of those proverbial "towns that time forgot." The crossroads community of old farmhouses was centered on a massive stone inn that had been built in 1718, and Dan's new home was only a stone's throw from the venerable landmark. The bungalow's setting was idyllic, with a view of fields and woods. The cozy house had three bedrooms, a parlor with a brick fireplace and a garage. There was even room for a garden just outside the kitchen door.[5]

Nan was ecstatic about her father's purchase and couldn't wait to move in. Wilna wasn't sure what to think. She dreaded being left alone again at the Hartranft House, but even so was taken aback when the Masons insisted that she come with them and make the bungalow her home as well. After mulling it over, anticipating a multitude of questions from her parents, she tentatively agreed. Predictably, on hearing the news the Herveys expressed their need to meet the Masons *immediately*. The fact that their daughter was moving in with strangers she had only recently met—and show business types at that—was an alarming prospect. Therefore, before Wilna could finalize her plans, she had to take Dan and Nan with her to Far Rockaway for an audience with William and Anna Hervey.[6]

The visit was a great success. Much to the relief (and perhaps surprise) of the Herveys, Dan Mason did not fulfill any of their expectations of stage and screen entertainers. He was in fact a cordial, sober, down-to-earth gentleman, well informed, well spoken and well mannered. He was a religious man—a practitioner of Christian Science—with a great deal of common sense, and not at all possessed of a celebrity ego. His daughter, Nan, though a bit rough around the edges, was sweet and guileless and possessed of the same rock-solid practicality as her father. With her parents' blessing, Wilna packed the Masons into her Dort and drove her new housemates back to Norristown. There, the trio loaded up her car, left behind the sparse rooms of the Hartranft House with their single light bulbs dangling from the ceiling, and moved to Audubon.

Recalling those days forty years later, Wilna wrote:

> [It was] one of the happiest periods of my life. . . . I think it was the blend of movie-making and the quiet settled charm of the surroundings in which we lived which created a sort of fay enchantment about those Audubon days. The movies brought the roaring twenties right to our doorstep, but also at that doorstep was the aura of a more ordered world. The very landscape, cherished as it had been by generations of industrious farmers, was a source of security and calm. Sometimes we moved in one of our worlds, sometimes in the other.[7]

Unmentioned in Wilna's dreamy recollections of those days was another important reason why both she and Nan would always cherish the memory of the little bungalow in rural Audubon, Pennsylvania. Though they hadn't quite realized it at the time, it was there that they fell in love.

As Nan got to know her father's co-star over the summer of 1920, her initial sense of insecurity slowly gave way to a wide-eyed and enthusiastic admiration for Wilna's talents and impressive range of knowledge. She also began to take much comfort in Wilna's gentle presence. As it became apparent that Nan was deeply mourning the recent loss of her mother, Wilna provided a sympathetic ear as well as a substantial shoulder to cry on when needed. Nan began to open up and the two girls began to bond. Just as Dan had taken on the inexperienced and bewildered Wilna as his special project at the studio, Wilna now took on Nan. In effect, after years of being the baby in her family, always protected and patronized, Wilna now assumed a very new role, that of "big sister." And it felt good.

Nan Mason, at the age of twenty-four, was surprisingly immature, especially for a woman who had been through two years of secretarial school and had a good job in an insurance firm. Her surviving letters from this period read as though they were penned by an awkward schoolgirl in her early teens. It was to Wilna's credit that, beyond Nan's clumsy presentation of self, she saw her new friend's enormous potential. She was a diamond in the rough and Wilna—ever the artist—set out to cut and polish that gem. Not that Nan necessarily wanted to be cut and polished. In fact, at first she resented many of Wilna's suggestions for her "improvement," as they only reinforced her lingering sense of inferiority. Wilna, however, gently and sweetly persisted. She began correcting Nan's spoken and written English, bought Nan new and badly needed underwear, and took her to the dentist to have her teeth fixed. She also tried—with limited success—to get Nan to tone down her extremely effusive manner of expression.[8]

Some of Nan's attempts to protect her ego resulted in unfortunate situations. Not yet aware of Wilna's propensity for compulsive, and occasionally expensive, gift giving, Nan casually claimed one day that she knew how to play the ukulele. When Wilna returned from visiting her parents the following Sunday night, she presented Nan with a new ukulele. Nan was forced to admit that she had stretched the truth. Wilna, who was naïve enough to be shocked that Nan had "fibbed," nevertheless began teaching her housemate a few basic chords and techniques. To her surprise and delight, Nan quickly became proficient on the instrument, and the two girls began singing in the evening after dinner.

Both the ukulele and Nan's ability to play it came in handy that summer when two of Wilna's friends came down from New York for a visit. Molly Pollock and Alexandrina Robertson Harris stayed for a week. After days spent swimming and horseback riding, the four girls stayed up late each night singing Molly's four-part harmonies to Nan's accompaniment. That Wilna's friends were an accomplished composer and a successful artist made a great impression on Nan, as did Wilna's insistence that Nan join them everywhere they went. By the time Molly and "Allie" went back to New York, Nan was calling Wilna by one of her youthful nicknames: "Woolie."[9]

During that first summer together in the bungalow, Wilna and Nan established the basic dynamics and routines of what would turn out to be their life together. Nan loved to keep house and, instinctively realizing that Wilna loved to be taken care of, did all the cleaning and shopping and cooking herself. When Katrinka and the Skipper arrived home from the studio, supper was ready. She made them breakfast and saw them off to work in the morning. Nan was, by all accounts, a very good cook. It was nothing fancy, no French recipes or gourmet preparations, just good down-to-earth American cuisine very well prepared. So it was natural that a garden should be planted to supply the household with fresh vegetables. But while all three of them dug and planted the

Wilna as Katrinka holding two puppies. In costume at the Betzwood studio, Wilna cuddles the two collie puppies, Teddy and Jess, that she and the Masons had just added to their household (in 1920).

garden, it was Nan who tended the plot and harvested the produce. Since all three of them loved animals, the Masons and their housemate convinced themselves that the garden needed protection and adopted two collie pups. There is also a parrot mentioned in a few letters, though just where this creature came from is uncertain. With Nan's cat and the bird already in residence, the addition of the two dogs brought the population of the bungalow to seven souls. The division of labor, the gardening, the profusion of pets, the evenings spent singing—all the elements of what would become Wilna and Nan's Woodstock lifestyle just a few years later—were in place by the fall of 1920.

At the end of the summer, with the first series of Toonerville films in the can and the studio closed, Wilna went back to New York to resume her art studies while Dan and Nan remained in their Audubon bungalow through the winter. Their idyllic summer ended with the bittersweet assumption by both of the girls that they were unlikely to see much of each other in the future. With her wedding now only months away, Nan expected to be living in Florida by the time Wilna returned to make more movies the following spring. It made their time together seem all the more special and Wilna's departure all the more poignant. Many tears were shed as Wilna packed up her Dort. The two girls promised to write.

And write they did, not just every week, but nearly every day without waiting for replies to their previous missives. None of the letters Wilna wrote to Nan during that fall and winter of 1920 has survived. However, many of Nan's letters have survived, and they make clear that the girls had formed an extraordinarily strong emotional bond in a span of only six months.

All of Nan's letters contain effusive expressions of her love for Wilna and indications that Wilna replied in kind. While much of Nan's rhapsodic (her own word) protestations of love might be written off as an intense schoolgirl crush, the volume of her expressed sentiments is remarkable and there are also occasional hints of eroticism. In late November, as Nan looked forward to a visit from Wilna at a time when her father would be away tending to business in Manhattan, she told Wilna of her feelings when thinking of her the previous evening:

> [I]t was a mighty good thing you were not near me, for I had a terrible naughty feeling—and I am trying so hard to lose it before my pal Woolie comes. . . . Woolie, my idea, of Dad going to New York and then you coming on—But do you think it safe? God, I might go mad yet from all the love I have stored down for you. You know it is "Safety First." What thinketh thou? But take it [from] me, Old dear, I am game.[10]

Nan's infatuation with Wilna and her willingness to express it physically and openly led at least one member of the Toonerville cast to warn Wilna about Nan's apparent "proclivities." When Wilna naïvely told Nan about the comments, Nan was hurt and defensive:

> I can just imagine how Betty said that about me being lonesome. I get her drift, very nicely, for I know what she thought. . . . It is just people like her, that cause one to get a bad name from a deep friendship feeling toward a girl. I would rather love as I do, then love like she does. But so the world goes, everybody for their taste.[11]

Wilna's reporting of the incident and Nan's response both suggest that neither of the girls had quite acknowledged the deep nature of the growing bond between them. With the expectation that the recent summer had been the only time they would ever live together, it is possible that each of them was holding back from coming to terms with their feelings, even to themselves.

Wilna's weeklong visit in early December 1920 left Nan feeling lonelier than ever. In mid-December, with the holidays approaching—Nan's second Christmas without her mother—she poured out her heart to Wilna in a long, rambling letter that makes clear just how much her emotional well-being now depended upon her friendship with Wilna:

> . . . dear child, you are so different from anybody I have ever met, out side of my dear mother, that treated me so sincere. Oh! Woolie, my heart isn't big enough for you . . . I can't put in words how I feel toward you child . . . I often think when I set at the fire place of you child, and say is it possible that Woolie, with all her Pals so near and dear to her really cares, as she does for me? I haven't a thing in common with you girl, in fact am way off in every way toward you, yet! fate has brought you around to care for me. . . . God! Woolie, you certainly have changed my life, and never could I pay you for all that you have done for me. I look at your picture and think, is it really me that has gotten a real true friend, that really cares for me at last.[12]

For Christmas, both of the Masons, and all of the pets, were the recipients of one of Wilna's typical showers of gifts. As little packages arrived day after day, Nan wept as she piled up the presents under the tree. She saved them all for opening on Christmas Day.

While Nan's Christmas of 1920 was relatively simple—the quiet company of her father and their pets, opening gifts in front of a log fire in the bungalow—Wilna's holiday was quite complicated. She had resumed her rollercoaster romance with Karoly Fulop upon her return to the Reiss studio in October. Perhaps because Karoly had an exhibition of his paintings on view at the Whitney Studio Club that November and December,[13] a circumstance that in his mind trumped Wilna's recent success in the movies, the star-crossed couple were enjoying a rare period of relative calm as the holidays approached. Karoly had, in fact, invited Wilna to come to his studio on Christmas Eve. Wilna was looking forward to this visit, but it was not to be.

On Christmas Eve, Wilna's mother urged her to stay home and Wilna reluctantly agreed. While her mother sat at the piano playing Beethoven, Wilna telephoned Karoly to let him know she would not be coming to his studio. But Karoly had no phone. The number he had given her was for the telephone in the adjoining studio, now locked up tight, its occupant gone for the holidays. Sensing that the persistently ringing phone might be his beloved trying to reach him, Karoly resorted to a desperate measure. He dashed up the stairs to the roof and, using the acrobatic skills that had served him well in his circus days in Hungary, jumped through the skylight of his friend's studio, landing on the floor amidst a shower of broken glass and bounding to the phone. With a cold wind whistling through the broken skylight and the sound of Beethoven wafting through the parlor of the Hervey mansion, Karoly and Wilna exchanged their Christmas greetings.[14]

Wilna spent most of the winter of 1920/21 at the Winold Reiss studio, basking in her newfound celebrity and enjoying the compliments of friends and acquaintances who had seen the Toonerville films. Bubi Schaeffer, soon on his way back to Germany where he would make his own first appearances on film, was especially enthusiastic about Wilna's evocation of Katrinka. Also soon to depart for his native Germany was one of Wilna's more unlikely fans, Ernst "Putzi" Hanfstaengel, the proprietor of Gallerie Hanfstaengel, where Winold Reiss had mounted his first one-man show the year before. Unlike Bubi Schaeffer, Putzi Hanfstaengel was not returning to Germany to appear in a film. Putzi was headed home to lend his support to Adolf Hitler's burgeoning National Socialist movement. Wilna's growing circle of friends was nothing if not eclectic.

With Wilna back in New York, Nan Mason's focus during those winter months was on assembling her trousseau in anticipation of her wedding, scheduled for the end of March. But the wedding never took place. On March 14th a telegram arrived at the Audubon bungalow. It was from Arthur's mother informing Nan that her fiancé had just died of pneumonia. "And so it was," Wilna later wrote, "for a very sad reason, that the three of us were together again in Audubon while the second series of Toonervilles was being made."[15]

The untimely death of Arthur Ryan brought Wilna and Nan back into each other's lives in a way that neither had anticipated and allowed them to pick up where they had left off the previous summer. Having lost her fiancé, Nan now leaned on Wilna for emotional support more than ever and the strong bond between them grew more intense. There is no indication that Nan ever again took an interest in or considered dating another man. Nan's father, relieved that Nan was not going away, actively encouraged her friendship with Wilna. Dan had by now developed his own deep affection for Wilna, to the point of regarding her as a second daughter and telling her as much. When the three of them were out in public and ran into someone Dan knew, he introduced both of the girls as his daughters with no further explanation.[16] He signed his letters to Wilna, "Your loving Dad." For the next couple of years, while living together in Dan Mason's household, Wilna and Nan would explain and define their relationship by calling themselves "sisters."

Almost as unexpected as Nan's continued presence in Audubon in April 1921 was the fact that Wilna went back to work at the movie studio with the blessing and encouragement of her parents. Though they didn't tell her at the time, the Herveys had actually gone to see the first of the Toonerville films when it played in Far Rockaway. With intense curiosity overriding both their distaste for the cinema and their fear of being seen in a movie theater, they had slipped quietly into the back of the house and nervously settled into their seats. When they found themselves roaring with laughter along with the rest of the audience, and later on receiving the congratulations of neighbors and friends on their daughter's performance, William and Anna Hervey did an about-face and enthusiastically embraced Wilna's movie career.[17]

The Herveys were finally beginning to accept the fact that the fragile and sensitive daughter they had protected for so long was morphing into an adventurous adult capable of making her own choices. Along with accepting Wilna's work as an actress, her parents gave their approval to another of her ambitions—to buy property so that she could settle down in Woodstock. In November of 1920, a month after returning home from the Betzwood motion picture studio, Wilna drove with her father to the Catskills to look over the possibilities. With her father pointing out that land was more reasonable outside of the village than within, Wilna used some of the proceeds of her summer of movie-making to buy a four-and-a-half-acre parcel of land in the hamlet of Bearsville, along the western boundary of Woodstock.[18] Over the next ten years this modest beachhead on what is now Route 212 would be expanded by further purchases until it had become a small real estate empire sprawling over much of Bearsville.

As the second round of filming the Toonerville Trolley films got underway, Wilna Hervey found her role as Katrinka so physically demanding that she devised a fitness routine to stay in shape. Since she had taught Nan how to ride a horse, the two went riding on the weekends and took advantage of opportunities to play football in the fields near the bungalow. Wilna was especially proud of her ability to kick the ball "to Hell and gone!" The girls also went swimming in the Schuylkill River that flowed along the southern border of the Betzwood studio grounds. One hot summer night, when they

impulsively went skinny-dipping under a full moon, Wilna dove in and swam under water to the middle of the river. When she suddenly surfaced, a frightened young couple in a canoe were staring at her in shock. To increase her already impressive strength, Wilna lifted weights, with Dan Mason showing her how to do it properly. She even went so far as to consult a professional fitness trainer.[19]

One weekend during a lull in filming, Wilna drove Nan up to Woodstock to show her the little piece of paradise she had claimed in the Catskills. The small rustic "studio" on Wilna's Bearsville property—a shambles that Dan Mason called a "$300 shack"—had no electricity, no indoor plumbing, and the only water came from a spring. Despite the notable inconveniences, which included sharing the one small bed and cooking over an open fire, Wilna and Nan enjoyed every minute of their weekend at Wilna's studio. That brief camping trip would ultimately prove to be as fateful as the untimely death of Nan's fiancé. Nan's reaction to Woodstock mirrored Wilna's response in the summer of 1918, albeit with even greater enthusiasm. It would not take much persuading a few years later to convince Nan to make her home there with Wilna.[20]

However, far from planning to settle down together in the fall of 1921, the girls were once again separated, this time by a distance of three thousand miles.

Nan Mason, Trying to Be Pals. *The two collies, now full grown (in 1921), attempt to get acquainted with Nan's reluctant tomcat. This tiny watercolor is the earliest known example of Nan's art work. It evokes the cozy atmosphere of the Audubon bungalow where she and Wilna lived with Nan's father—and hints at the artistic potential that would later blossom in Woodstock.*

CHAPTER 6

California

Opposite: The Plum Centerpedes. Cast and crew of the Plum Center Comedies are featured in this publicity flyer issued when the first of the Pop Tuttle films was being made in 1922. Dan and Wilna's equine co-star, "Wildfire," was actually on his way to the glue factory when the studio's casting agent discovered his talent for looking decrepit.

Up against daunting competition, the Toonerville Trolley films were successful, but not successful enough. With more than two thousand comedy films released in the United States in 1920 and 1921, Hollywood was offering everything from the frenzied slapstick of the Mack Sennett productions to the increasingly brilliant work of comic geniuses like Charlie Chaplin, Buster Keaton and Harold Lloyd. Popular stars such as "Fatty" Arbuckle, Lloyd Hamilton, Mabel Normand, Snub Pollard and Charley Chase continued to entertain movie audiences, as they had for years. In the end, the little studio in the Philadelphia suburbs and its quaint cartoons-come-to-life could not survive. For the businessmen who had bought the Betzwood studio as an investment and were focused more on the bottom line than on the opinions of movie critics, the little movie factory was slowly becoming a liability. In midsummer 1921, Wolf Brothers, Inc. abruptly suspended production and closed the Betzwood studio. Only six of the intended twenty-four new films had been made. The sudden halt in movie-making sent all of the studio's employees, from directors to lab technicians, scattering. "Everyone was in such a hurry . . . that we didn't even have a farewell party," Wilna remembered. When Dan Mason visited the studio in late September to return a tarpaulin he had borrowed for his house, he reported finding the once bustling studio "quiet as a cemetery."[1]

Dan's role as the Toonerville Skipper had brought him more professional acclaim and a higher salary than any other part he had played in his half-century career, and he was not willing to have it all taken away so quickly. Convinced that there was a lot of mileage left in the Toonerville concept and the folksy characterizations he and Wilna had so successfully crafted, Dan began looking for ways to continue making the films. If the Betzwood investors were no longer willing to fund Fox's comedies, perhaps more savvy producers elsewhere in the movie industry could be persuaded to do so. After a flurry of letters, phone calls and visits to New York City to meet with Fontaine Fox and the head of First National Pictures, Dan headed to California. He told Wilna that he would set up new Toonerville productions, arrange for her to be paid a good salary and send for

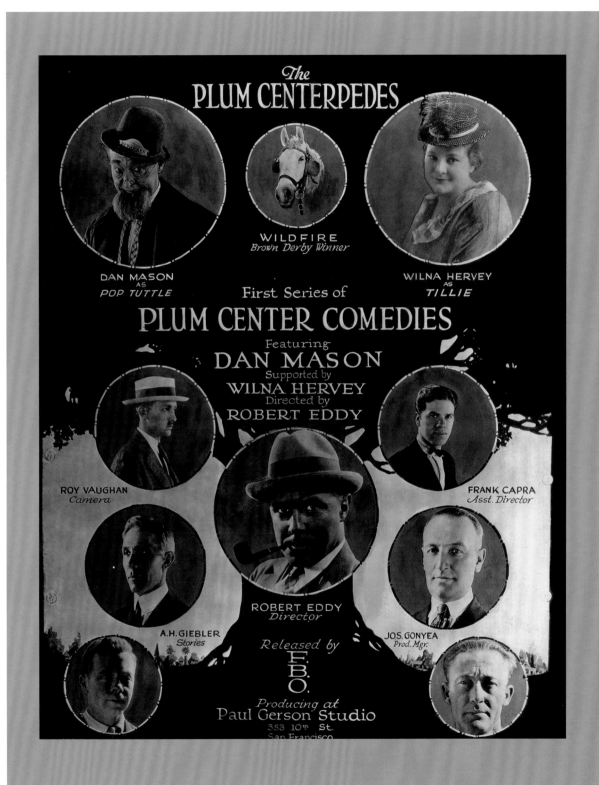

Above: Wilna Hervey and Dan Mason as Tillie Olson and Pop Tuttle. The characters that Wilna and Dan played in the Plum Center Comedies mirrored those they had portrayed in the Toonerville films, but with different names. The sight gag of Wilna lugging around a heavy trunk was carried over from Katrinka to Tillie.

Below: Pop Tuttle's One Horse Play. Pop Tuttle as Richard III and Tillie Olson as Ophelia (yes, we know—wrong play!) adjust the lighting in the Plum Center Theater before going up on stage. Nan Mason can be seen in the audience just below Wilna and looking up at her father. It was in this film that Wilna suffered an unexpected balcony collapse on camera and Nan endured a cascade of soot dumped on her head as she watched the show.

her. In early October, Dan closed up the Audubon bungalow and, accompanied by his daughter, two collies, a cat and a parrot, boarded a train for California. The weeklong journey across the continent in a Pullman stateroom with a menagerie of spoiled pets used to having the run of the house must have afforded the Masons more drama, thrills and raw comedy than any film Dan ever made.

With her friends on their way to California, Wilna Hervey retreated briefly to her studio in Bearsville, bought five more acres of land, then returned to the comfort of the Winold Reiss studio—and the discomfort of Karoly Fulop. Her possessive Hungarian suitor was magnanimous, convinced that the dissolution of the Betzwood Film Company meant that his favorite Amazon was now finished with the movies and would never abandon him again. In the interest of international relations, Wilna avoided mentioning that Dan Mason was already plotting her return to the silver screen from his outpost in Hollywood.[2]

Left: Dan Mason and Wilna Hervey in Pop Tuttle's One Horse Play. *As Plum Center's leading thespians take to the stage, Pop Tuttle's tights are ripped, his battered crown is cockeyed, the backdrop is awful and Tillie Olson is wearing old, worn-out work shoes under her formal gown. Scenes like this make it easy to see why Wilna considered movie making to be such fun.*

Above: Eek, a mouse! Nan plays a Plum Center character frightened by a mouse while her father, as Pop Tuttle, reacts with alarm at the sight of the rodent. When she wasn't home cleaning and cooking and tending to the pets, Nan enjoyed taking on minor roles in the Plum Center Comedies. Unfortunately none of the films she appeared in has survived.

In January 1922, as Wilna relaxed with her parents amidst the Victorian trappings of their winter retreat, the exclusive Pine Forest Inn in Summerville, South Carolina, she received a telegram from Dan:

> Arranging to make two series of pictures—want you with me—can get you $250 per week—Hope you will accept and start for California when I wire the word "come." Long to have you with us. Love from us all. Dan.[3]

Wilna was soon on her way to Los Angeles for a reunion with her second family and a fresh start to her movie career. She would be in California for more than a year, and would not see Karoly again for nearly six years. Though they would occasionally write, Wilna would make no further attempt at maintaining a romantic relationship.

Dan Mason's brief telegram left out an important fact. Wilna was traveling to the west coast not to make more Toonerville films but to appear in a wholly new series that was the product of Dan's fertile imagination. Unable to convince Fontaine Fox to continue the Toonerville series, Dan had opted to honor the films that he and Wilna had recently made with the sincerest form of flattery: imitation. In the films Dan envisioned, Toonerville would become Plum Center, and the rural characters who lived there, while identical in appearance and personality to the beloved denizens of Fox's outpost in the boondocks, would all have different names. Dan Mason would portray Pop Tuttle, the irascible and eccentric driver of a dilapidated horse-drawn "bus" that took commuters to and from the train depot. To avoid legal problems with Fontaine Fox, there would be no trolley. Wilna would play Tillie Olson, a large and utterly clueless Swedish girl hired by Pop Tuttle to do odd jobs. The story lines and situations that Dan and the writers were working on were essentially a continuation of the Toonerville saga, prohibition jokes and all. Robert Eddy, who had directed many of the Toonervilles, was on board as well, to take charge of the Plum Center films.

One significant difference in the Plum Center Comedies was that Wilna was featured as Dan's co-star and enjoyed much more screen time than previously. While Katrinka had been only one of several characters in the Toonerville stories, and was occasionally marginalized, Tillie was a central figure around whom the films revolved. Even after learning that her salary would actually be one hundred and fifty a week and not two fifty, Wilna reveled in this expansion of her onscreen time. Wilna was also credited with her real family name for the first time. As the Plum Center films were to be produced by the Paul Gerson Studio in San Francisco, Wilna and the Masons left Los Angeles shortly after Wilna's arrival, boarding the Sunset Limited for the trip north.

The high spirits and excitement that everyone felt as they embarked on their new movie-making venture were suddenly dashed shortly after production began on the first Pop Tuttle comedy. On March 17th, as Wilna and Dan returned from the studio, they found Nan standing in the doorway crying, a telegram in her hand. Wilna's mother had died of a heart attack that morning. With the funeral scheduled for only two days later, there was no way for Wilna to return to Far Rockaway. The film production schedule made a two-week round trip to New York by rail impossible. Wilna had no choice but to remain in San Francisco and obey the old theatrical adage "the show must go on." With Dan's help and counsel— he had twice been compelled to go on with a show after losing an infant son while on tour—Wilna dug deep for the courage and discipline it took to be a trouper. Her grief

Nan Mason, Still Life Study. *It was in California in 1922 that Nan's considerable artistic talent began to assert itself. Her skill, even without formal training, is evident in this and other works she created while her father and Wilna were making the Plum Center Comedies.*

compounded by the daily arrival of her mother's last letters for an entire week after her death, Wilna nevertheless donned her costume and makeup each day and tried to "act silly" for the camera. That she wasn't always successful at overcoming her distress is suggested by the fact that in the very first film they shot—*Pop Tuttle's Movie Queen*—Wilna has only a cameo role despite her billing as one of the stars. She would later admit to Winold Reiss that making the first three movies in the new series had been extremely difficult for her.[4]

Anna Hervey's will directed that her fortune be divided equally among her four children. Though it took some time for the legal details to be worked out and a trust fund set up for the purpose, Wilna and her siblings each ended up inheriting something in the neighborhood of half a million dollars. In today's money, that would come to six and a half million. Wilna Hervey was now a very wealthy young movie star. For the next ten years, she would sail through life assuming that her financial resources were unlimited.[5]

As with the Toonerville films, the exteriors for the Plum Center Comedies needed to be shot in a quaint rural community, and the sleepy hamlet of Belmont, about twenty-five miles south of San Francisco, was chosen as the home of Pop Tuttle and Tillie Olson. With an hour-long commute in director Robert Eddy's Cadillac a near daily necessity, a familiar routine born of the Audubon days reasserted itself. Dan and Wilna were up and out early in the morning while Nan cleaned, shopped, cooked, exercised the dogs, played with the cat and had dinner on the table when the weary "Plum Centerpedes" rolled in with the evening fog.

On occasion, however, Nan joined her father and Wilna on location or at the Gerson studio in San Francisco to make her own appearances in the films as an extra. There were days when she regretted accepting their invitation. During one scene, set in a theater where Pop Tuttle and Tillie were acting out a fractured version of Shakespeare, a stovepipe directly above Nan was rigged to break and dump three shovelfuls of soot on her head. As per practice when filming comedy in those days, she was not warned of this ahead of time. In another film, she wore a hat surmounted by a bird, which a hunter was to mistake for the real thing and shoot. A small explosive charge in the hat, intended to create the comic effect of the hat exploding, set fire to her hair, removed her eyebrows and singed her ears. Her worst cinematic experience came when she was obliged to play the part of an outraged woman who beats Pop Tuttle over the head with her umbrella. Following Dan's instructions—"Nannie, please don't be afraid to hit me with the umbrella. Make it real. Hit me *hard* and I will duck"—Nan laid into her father with athletic abandon before realizing to her horror that there were rivulets of blood pouring down his face.[6] Nan's mishaps were not the only accidents that befell the cast of the Plum Center Comedies. Wilna suffered a balcony collapse on camera only to discover that the director liked it so much she had to repeat it later that day. Dan Mason was accidentally catapulted high into the air by a sight gag gone very wrong. He hit the asphalt with such a sickening thud that it made Wilna physically ill. Only his years of experience taking pratfalls saved the sixty-eight-year-old actor from serious injury.[7]

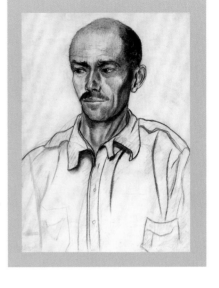

Nan Mason, Unidentified Man. *One of the several ethnic portraits Nan drew in California, this sketch hints of Winold Reiss's influence in both her subject matter and her direct approach. It is obvious that Wilna had been adding her advice and encouragement to Nan's early experiments as an artist.*

Nan Mason and Wilna Hervey with Molly Pollock and Frank Capra. Molly had come to San Francisco from New York in March 1922 to console Wilna after her mother died. She stayed a month and even played a bit part in one of the Plum Center films. She was very impressed by the young assistant director whose long and distinguished career was just beginning.

Needing help managing the productions, Robert Eddy hired an affable young Sicilian immigrant to work with him as assistant director. His name was Frank Capra. "I think we all sensed that he was slated for 'the big time'," Wilna recalled. "[H]e had that quality of giving confidence to others, something no one needed more than I." Wilna and Capra hit it off, and it was not long before Capra and the studio cameraman, Roy Vaughn, were frequent visitors to the Mason–Hervey household for dinner and an evening of singing in four-part harmony to Nan's ukulele accompaniments. Frank Capra would become their lifelong friend.[8]

In late spring 1922 Wilna took advantage of a brief hiatus in filming to travel south along the California coast to visit her brother, Thomas V. Cator, and his family. She insisted that Nan come along. Thomas Cator, an innovative and highly regarded composer, lived in Carmel-by-the-Sea. Neither of the girls had ever been to Carmel before and they were stunned by the beauty of the charming little "village in the forest" perched above the Pacific, reacting very much as they both had to their initial exposure to Woodstock. Like Woodstock, Carmel was a very small community in those days, and largely populated by artists, composers, writers and other creative types. The native Monterey pines were everywhere, as they are today. The large Cator house at the corner of Lopez Avenue and Fourth Avenue had a beautiful view of the sea and was nestled close to a hill of pine and eucalyptus trees. Never without her sketchbooks and watercolors, Wilna soon began seeking out vantage points above the sea where she might try to capture the remarkable views that stretched out in all directions. She finished several small works and was even paid the compliment of having one of them stolen from her.[9]

It was during their visit to Carmel that Nan Mason decided to become a professional artist. Each time Wilna went out to the cliffs overlooking the Pacific to paint, Nan went along, but had nothing to do while she waited. One day Wilna encouraged her to take the sketchbook and draw a nearby "ghost tree." When she returned two hours later, Wilna was astonished to see the sketch Nan had made. "I nearly fell off the rock into the sea," she remembered. "It was better than I could have done!"[10] And so began the art career of Nan Mason. In subsequent months, with Wilna urging her on, Nan continued to draw and also took up painting. As can be seen from several of her surviving charcoal sketches done in 1924, before she had received any professional training, Nan was possessed of considerable natural talent.

The twelfth and final Plum Center Comedy was completed on January 27th, 1923. Before leaving California, Wilna headed back to Carmel and purchased three small plots in a new development being laid out on the edge of the village. "Carmel is a marvelous place to paint and I will go there again some day," she wrote to Winold Reiss. A few days later, the Masons, Wilna and their family circus were on a train headed for the east coast.[11] However, with Dan and his daughter going to check on their bungalow in Audubon, Pennsylvania, and Wilna going to her family home in Far Rockaway, the girls found themselves apart once again. This separation—after living together for a full year—was especially difficult. Wilna and Nan planned to visit between New York and Pennsylvania as much as possible, but a few months later Dan abruptly took Nan and the menagerie back to Los Angeles with him, eliminating any possibility of the hoped-for visits. While this relocation afforded Dan opportunities for securing character roles in Hollywood films, it also brought the veteran trouper the persistent headache of dealing with a very unhappy, lonely and uncharacteristically irritable daughter. "Have often wished I had let Nannie remain with you together with Teddy and Jess [the two collies], and have all come out here later," Dan wrote to Wilna from Los Angeles in June. "You are very near and dear to Nannie. Your influence with her is even more than if you were sisters."[12] Fortunately for all concerned, this separation did not last long. After spending the summer at her studio in Bearsville, where she purchased another two parcels of land, Wilna headed back to California, hoping to obtain further work in the movies and, more importantly, to be reunited with Nan. Beyond that September of 1923, Wilna Hervey and Nan Mason would never again be separated until Wilna's death in 1979.[13]

Wilna's success in the Toonerville and Plum Center pictures had given her an appetite for more movie work. She loved appearing before the camera, and though she really didn't need more money—having inherited such a large nest egg from her mother—she loved the way cash was thrown at her simply for having fun. It was discretionary money that she could do with as she pleased. But in Hollywood that fall all she managed to land was an uncredited bit part in Mary Pickford's production of *Rosita*[14]—and it had been hard to come by. By the end of the year, Wilna was forced to come to terms with the fact that there just weren't that many parts available for an actress of her size. Meanwhile, Nan's enthusiasm for drawing and painting was making Wilna reconsider the toll her intensive movie work of recent years was taking on her own artistic ambitions, a pursuit she cared about deeply.

In December, while Dan Mason was away in northern California for an extended movie shoot, Wilna and Nan had time to sit around, openly smoke their forbidden cigarettes and talk more freely than they could in front of Nan's father. By the time Dan returned to Hollywood, his girls had come to a momentous decision. Together, the two of them would move back east to Bearsville in the spring. They would build themselves a proper house on Wilna's property and focus their energies on becoming professional artists.

CHAPTER 7

Settling Down

It was early June when Wilna and Nan, and Nan's cat, finally settled into Wilna's glorified shack in Bearsville. A severe gallbladder attack put Wilna out of commission in March and delayed their move for several months.[1] Throughout her life Wilna would often experience bouts of illness, some of them quite serious, when compelled to deal with the stress of personal milestones. Nursing Wilna back to health under such circumstances would become part of Nan's routine.

Up until now the two girls had lived together as sisters under Dan Mason's roof, their close friendship defined by the fact that they were two young women thrown together by the circumstances of movie-making. Now, for the first time since they met, they were living together because they had chosen to do so, independently and on their own. Furthermore, they had mutually chosen the pursuit of art as the life path they would follow together. Nan's father seems to have understood the significance of their decision to establish a home together, and he gave them his blessing in a touching letter written only a week after their arrival in Bearsville:

> I am happy when I know you are both happy. I want to see that harmony grow and expand in your two lives. Both giving and taking for your mutual welfare and happiness. Love is the great vital force. Love is life, without it life is a void. Poor indeed is the man or woman who do not or never have known true love.[2]

Wilna celebrated her return to the Catskills by purchasing another one-and-a-half-acre parcel of land in Bearsville, adding to the considerable collection of lots she now owned along the Bearsville–Shady Road. On several of these properties she now constructed modest cabins, or "studios," as she would always call them, intending to rent them to the influx of artists who swelled the population of Woodstock each summer. Her own experience of living with Molly Pollock in the loft of a barn in the summer of 1918 had convinced her that this would be a good way to generate income. Wilna's small studios were rustic but well constructed, as one surviving photo testifies. Compared to the conditions in which some artists lived on the Maverick, they were downright palatial.

Wilna poses beside one of her artist studios under construction in Bearsville. The little rental cottages she had built were quite rustic; they were not insulated and the fireplace would have been the primary source of heat.

In addition to the rental cabins, Wilna and Nan arranged for the construction of their first home that summer. Their cottage had one large living area dominated by a stone fireplace, a modest kitchen with a wood-burning stove and extra-high counters, a bedroom too small for anything more than one double bed, and a loft for storage. The "studio," as Wilna would describe it, was supplied with water by a pipe running from a nearby spring to which Wilna had secured the rights. However, in a somewhat extravagant gesture for Bearsville in those days, a stone cesspool and state-of-the-art septic system was installed to serve the primitive bathroom tucked into what had started out as a back porch. With no electric service available, they relied on kerosene lamps and candles at night. Both agreed it was heaven.

The financing of these construction projects was made possible, for the most part, by the generous monthly payments Wilna received from the Hervey Post Trust. Her late mother's considerable fortune (partially inherited from her aunt, Hannah Post) had been placed in a trust that doled out regular checks to Anna Hervey's four children. Wilna's father and her sister Eleanor managed the trust. The Hervey Post Trust, combined with whatever rentals Wilna could generate from her Bearsville studios, provided Wilna with the income she lived on. Nan's income was largely dependent upon the monthly allowance her father sent her. With Dan Mason making princely salaries as a popular character actor in Hollywood, and living extremely frugally, he was able to send his daughter a tidy sum each month and extra when she needed it.

For Nan, one of the genuine thrills of her first full summer in the Catskills was meeting all of Wilna's artist friends. By now, the greater Woodstock area had a hundred or so artists in residence for at least part of the year, and Wilna was already well acquainted with many of the most prominent. Exactly how and when Wilna met the several Woodstock artists who would become her lifelong friends is unknown, but bonds with Eugene and Elsie Speicher, Kaj and Georgina Klitgaard, Charles Rosen, Henry Lee

Wilna and Nan build their first home together. The cozy "studio" cottage, constructed on Wilna's original parcel of land in Bearsville, New York, would be their home from 1924 to 1928, and later from 1942 to 1960.

The old dry stone wall in the foreground was recycled for the foundation and fireplace.

At the end of a workday, Wilna checks on the progress of the stonemasons.

and Aileen McFee, Paul and Caroline Rohland, John Carroll, and Clarence McCarthy seem to have been forged early on. By 1924, when she and Nan set up house, Wilna had spent the better part of four summers in Woodstock, interacting with the art community in a variety of ways. Even when she hadn't been in town, "Katrinka" and "Tillie Olson" had been. During the summers of 1921, 1922 and 1923, Wilna's Toonerville and Plum Center films ran in local theaters and were advertised in the *Kingston Daily Freeman*, the paper that the artists relied upon for their news. Wilna, and her avoirdupois, were sufficiently well known in the Woodstock community by 1921 that Earle B. Winslow could portray her clambering into a public transport in his humorous painting *The Woodstock Bus*, confident that the local cognoscenti would get the joke. Thus Wilna was already a prominent figure in 1924, with some measure of celebrity status.

Thanks to Wilna's close friendship with Winold Reiss, who was once again teaching in Woodstock the summer they moved to Bearsville, she and Nan met other artists as well, including the beautiful young Erika Lohmann, Reiss's frequent companion since his divorce from Henriette in 1923. All of Wilna's Woodstock friends were happy to welcome Nan into their lives. As they got to know her and came to an appreciation of her artistic and musical talents, as well as her level-headedness and unfailing good humor, Nan became a welcome companion and even a confidante. Early on, their friends began to refer to Wilna and Nan as "the Big Girls," and the name stuck. They would be the Big Girls, or just "the girls," to their friends and colleagues well into old age.

Wilna and Nan were not the first same-sex couple to settle down in Woodstock to pursue artistic careers. During her earliest sojourns in the valley, when she was studying with the Art Students League, Wilna had learned of a unique enclave of independent artistic women, called the Blue Dome Fraternity, who had been living and working together for years just up the road from Bearsville in the hamlet of Shady. Led by the accomplished painter and teacher Dewing Woodward and her companion, Louise Johnson, the Blue

Nan can be seen at the far left in this photo taken by Wilna as the roof was being installed. *The nearly finished cottage sits at the base of the slope that would eventually be covered in trees. At the top of the slope is Cooper Lake Road.*

Nan Mason, Wilna Hervey, Winold Reiss, Hans Reiss, Erika Lohmann and Otto Baumgarten in Bearsville. Reiss was teaching in Woodstock in the summer of 1924 and introduced Wilna and Nan to the beautiful young artist Erika Lohmann, his frequent companion after his divorce in 1923.

Wilna and Nan at the Maverick Festival, 1924. The young woman is unidentified, but the man on the left is artist Clarence McCarthy, a close friend of the girls for many years. We know that grapes were part of their lunch that day. Fifty years later, Nan recalled throwing them at everyone after she'd had a few drinks.

Dome group—supposedly named for the French-inspired technique of using sheets of blue gauze to filter the sunlight when they worked outdoors—had scandalized the locals and even several of the Woodstock artists some years earlier by posing fully nude female figures *en plein air* during the art lessons they offered to beginners and advanced painters alike.[3]

However, by 1920, the year Wilna bought her first property in Bearsville, less than two miles from the former home of Woodward and Johnson, the Blue Dome Fellowship (as they later preferred to be known) had relocated to Florida, where they added a decorating business to their art school. Though Woodward and Johnson would retain some ties to Woodstock into the early twenties, even planting more trees on their property in Shady in 1922, they had pulled up stakes by the time Wilna and Nan came to put down roots in 1924.[4]

Even if the two couples were not fated to be friends or confrères, the Blue Dome pioneers had helped pave the way for the young homesteaders as a committed couple, at least within the community of artists. But even among the locals, who were often wary of artistic newcomers and their unconventional ways, Wilna and Nan encountered no known hostility. In fact, they established long-term friendships with a couple of their Bearsville neighbors, some of whom represented families that had been in the valley for generations and had no connections whatever to the world of writers and painters. Wilna's innocent demeanor and Nan's perpetual smile coupled with their total lack of pretension may have been helpful in this regard. So may have Wilna's willingness to pay often-inflated prices for local real estate. In general, the girls were well received in their adopted town, and any notoriety they acquired arose from issues unrelated to the fact that they were life partners.

Another treat for Nan that first summer in Woodstock was the annual Maverick Festival, now in its tenth year, on the day of the August full moon. Wilna and Nan attended wearing clown suits, a costume choice that would become their signature for many moons to come. One of Nan's fond memories of that day, some fifty years later, was of getting drunk and throwing grapes at everyone. The Maverick Festival that year featured a production of the play *The Ark Royale*, staged on an eighty-foot-long pirate ship with sixty-foot-tall masts, built for the occasion by Walter Steinhilber, who also wrote the drama. To the astonishment and delight of the audience gathered in the open-air theater, the ship was burned down during the finale of the play.[5]

The leaves had already begun to turn when Dan Mason and the family's two well-traveled collies arrived from California for a brief visit in late September 1924. During his stay, Dan issued his usual exhortations for thrift and the exercise of common sense, and unloaded the two rambunctious dogs that had become a burden to him when he had to work on location. He also financed Nan's purchase of her own piece of property, a two-acre plot along Cooper Lake Road, adjoining one of Wilna's recent purchases. The girls' growing real estate empire now stretched between the two roads leading north out of Bearsville. Nan's purchase of land alongside Wilna's bore symbolic weight as a gesture that spoke of her commitment to their partnership. Late in October, Wilna bought two more properties, including the road now known as Ballantine Lane, to provide access to a couple of her otherwise land-locked parcels.[6]

Earle B. Winslow, The Woodstock Bus. *Oil painting. That's Wilna disappearing into the bus as it picks up fares on the village green in this droll rendering from 1921. The image of this quaint vehicle groaning under Wilna's weight calls to mind the scenes of Powerful Katrinka boarding the Toonerville Trolley being filmed that same year.*

The Growth of the Soil

The New York state census for 1925 lists Wilna Hervey as a farmer and Nan Mason as a housewife. While this brief entry provides an unsurprising clue to the inner dynamics of their relationship, it also tells us that Wilna and Nan were not devoting all of their time and energy to art as they had originally planned. During the winter of 1924/25, Wilna had read the 1920 Nobel Prize-winning novel *The Growth of the Soil*, and was captivated by Knut Hamsun's epic tale of an intrepid settler who hikes deep into the remote forests of Norway and, with his loyal common-law wife, transforms a Spartan homestead into a prosperous farm. Identifying with the main character, Isak, and using the novel as a kind of script for a real-life dramatic role, Wilna declared her desire to "get back to the earth" and began plotting an ambitious scheme that would make her and Nan virtually self-sufficient while providing them with another source of income. Always willing to follow Wilna's lead, Nan was enthusiastically in agreement with this plan. Their large garden of 1924 was greatly expanded in 1925 and again in 1926. Wilna also purchased chickens, ducks and geese with the intention of selling eggs and fowl, a cow to provide milk and a horse to pull the plow. To accommodate the livestock, they built a small barn, twenty by thirty feet, in the summer of 1925, along with a large, heated chicken coop. As their first foray into animal husbandry, the intrepid farmers also acquired another dog, a female collie they hoped to breed with their two male collies with the intention of selling the puppies. The "boys" were only too happy to cooperate.[1]

From his home in Los Angeles, Dan Mason watched the Bearsville homestead grow through the lens of the near-daily letters that the three of them exchanged, and was delighted with the girls' decision to invest their energies in farming. The healthy benefits of fresh food and fresh air appealed to him almost as much as the money-saving aspects of growing one's own groceries. Since the girls were already pleading with him to retire and come to live with them, Dan suggested that he would be willing to help finance the purchase of an even larger property that they could all farm together. Not surprisingly, Wilna already had her eye on the perfect parcel. Now in possession of much of the land

Nan Mason, Along the Hudson: River Landscape. *Nan began formal art training almost immediately upon arriving in Woodstock in 1924. This atmospheric view of the Hudson River, done while she was studying under George Bellows, is Nan's earliest surviving oil painting and the earliest known work from her Woodstock years.*

between the state road (Route 212) and the narrow unpaved country lane known as Cooper Lake Road, Wilna looked to expand her fiefdom's borders into territories not yet conquered. West of Cooper Lake Road, high on a hill, stood an old farmstead known locally as Treasure Farm. When Dan came east in August 1926, to play a role in a film being shot in New York City, he paid a brief visit to Bearsville and the girls took him to see the property. Impressed by the fact that they were already selling their own produce, eggs, milk and Nan's homemade cheese to local residents, Dan was encouraged by the possibilities. Before he went back to New York City he wrote out a check to put money down on the "farm on the hill."[2]

Dan Mason was not without his concerns, however. There were frequent lapses of common sense innocently reported in the girls' letters, and some of the things he had seen in person during his visit worried him. Wilna and Nan were taking on more animals than they could easily handle, including a litter of collie puppies that, while very cute, were not so cute that anyone actually wanted to buy them. "One cow, the horse and a few chickens would have been more than enough," he scolded, once he'd had time to think about it. He had a hunch—correct, as it turned out—that they might be tempted to run off during the winter, something farmers simply cannot do.[3]

One development with which Dan could not quarrel was Nan's hard work and devotion to her art training. Nan Mason seems to have made a more serious effort than Wilna to stay focused on developing her skills, even with all the distractions of farming. Within weeks of their arrival in June 1924, she had begun taking art lessons from one of the most prominent Woodstock artists, George Bellows. Nan's initial lessons with Bellows went quite well. He praised one of her drawings of an African-American subject as having "all of Africa in it!"[4] Her evolution as a landscape painter also owed much to his influence. Wilna was so proud of Nan's rapid advancement that she wrote a glowing letter to Dan, suggesting that Nan's work was better than her own. "I am afraid you are belittling your own ability," Dan Mason sweetly replied. "One thing is certain, were it not for you she would not now be so engaged, so a great big share of credit must go to you."[5]

Charles Rosen at the Maverick Festival. A serious and thoughtful artist and a highly regarded teacher, Charles Rosen had an impish sense of humor and a well-developed sense of the absurd. Abandoning his usual professorial demeanor for the 1924 Maverick Festival, Rosen dressed as a combination ballerina/Cupid, brandishing a wooden clothes hanger as a bow. His keen sense of fun endeared him to Wilna and Nan early on.

When George Bellows died unexpectedly from a burst appendix in January 1925, Nan became a student of one of Woodstock's most beloved artists, Charles Rosen, and her landscapes began to take on some of the modernist grounding in solid geometry that characterized Rosen's Woodstock work. Perhaps attracted to the harbor at Rondout, near Kingston, by Rosen's own work at that location, Nan produced a print of boats moored there that shows just how much she was influenced by her mentor's approach. Rosen and Nan rapidly developed a close friendship that would survive until his death a quarter of a century later. It is easy to see how they would hit it off. Like Nan, Rosen was good-natured, down to earth and always ready with a smile. During the year that Nan began her studies with him, Rosen dressed as a ballerina for the annual Maverick Festival, proudly flaunting his knobby knees beneath his fluffy tutu. That gesture, if nothing else, would have endeared him to Nan and her silent-film comedienne partner.

An Appetite For Art

When Dan Mason finished his film in New York City in late August 1926, he stopped in Bearsville once more before returning to California. There, his girls gave him a surprise that haunted him all the way back to Hollywood. In the four weeks since he had last seen them, they had decided to spend the next six months in Europe, touring the major cities and visiting all of the famous art museums. Though he must have been appalled at their decision to leave their farm and board all of their livestock with friends and neighbors through the winter, Dan opted to tread lightly. Having recently touched off a storm of weeping and anxiety attacks with some pointed criticism of their approach to farm management, he now chose to focus solely on his concerns for their well-being and safety.

The mercurial decision to go to Europe almost certainly originated with Wilna, and Nan as usual had been only too happy to concur. Wilna had already begun making plans, using the legendary Thomas Cook travel agency to make all the necessary arrangements. She had spared no expense, reasoning that two young women traveling alone would be much safer traveling first class. Cook's agents would meet them at every juncture throughout the trip, escort them to and from arrival and departure points, handle their luggage and transport them to their posh hotels. Personal guided tours—on occasion in limousines and extending over two days—would be provided as well. The company would even see to paying all tips and gratuities, to spare them the "inconvenience."

Proceeds from the butter, eggs and produce the two newly minted farmers had been peddling by horse and cart along the roads and byways of Bearsville could not support such extravagance, and it is likely that Wilna financed most of the trip herself. In addition to the fat checks she was receiving from the Hervey Post Trust, Wilna had recently inherited nearly nineteen thousand dollars from her father, who had died in October 1925. Nan probably paid what she could out of her earnings—and the monthly support that her father provided.[1]

In late October, with the harvest in, all the animals—including half a dozen unsold and rapidly growing puppies—were farmed out to neighbors and Nan's beloved old

With loads of love
from your "Daughter" -
Florence,
Italy
12/19/36

tomcat was deposited in the home of a friend. After a shopping spree in New York City to outfit themselves for the journey, Wilna and Nan boarded the French liner *Rochambeau* and sailed to Europe.

Their first stop was Paris, where they spent most of the month of November. The cultural shock was cushioned by the fact that they both had some familiarity with the French language and had, as well, the names and addresses of several friends of friends living there. For the most part, however, they were on their own to explore the city's cultural offerings and settle into the pattern of everyday life in Paris. It rained much more than they expected but they didn't let the damp and chill keep them from taking long walks through the city's streets.

By the time they left Paris, Wilna and Nan had established the routine they would follow in each of the cities they visited during their trip. In pursuit of fine art, they sought out every available museum, palace and church that housed the works they had come to study, and took note of the great wonders of architecture and sculpture as well. They made frequent stops to sketch scenic vistas, and Wilna—ever the devoted student of Winold Reiss—often sketched the faces of "types" she saw on the streets. As the weeks went by, their portfolios began to bulge with hundreds of sketches.

Bulges began to assert themselves in less welcome locations as well. It was not lost on the young gourmands that the most fattening of the fine arts—*haute cuisine*—was being showcased everywhere. As with the works on canvas they devoured with such enthusiasm, the masterpieces crafted in the kitchens of Paris, Florence, Venice and Rome were closely studied, every detail absorbed.

Wilna with Anna Reiss, mother of Winold Reiss. One of the highlights of Wilna and Nan's European adventure was their visit with Winold Reiss's mother and sister in Kirchzarten, Germany. Anna Reiss didn't speak English but her home cooking spoke volumes to her visitors' stomachs . . . and hearts.

Through the first nine weeks of their journey, Wilna and Nan ate grand lunches and splendid dinners virtually every day. Some of the menus impressed them so much they saved them as keepsakes. Not that they were ever in danger of losing the memory of those meals. No amount of walking the miles of city streets or the long galleries of venerable museums could burn off as many calories as they encountered and gleefully accepted on a daily basis. Even before they left Paris, both of the well-dressed American travelers were aware of an annoying tightness in their stylish new clothing.

Wilna had promised Winold Reiss that she would visit his mother. So, before heading down into Italy where they hoped to escape the chill and incessant rain of Paris, the girls boarded a train for Germany. The day Wilna and Nan spent at the Reiss family home was one of the highlights of their trip. Anna Reiss spoke no English, so after an hour of Wilna's entertaining but futile attempts to communicate through pantomime and picture drawing, a local woman was recruited to translate for them. Before they left at the end of the day, die Mutti Reiss presented both Wilna and Nan with drawings done by Winold Reiss's late father, Fritz, a gesture that deeply touched them.[2]

▲ ▲ ▲

There was no car or taxi awaiting the girls when they disembarked from their train in Venice on the evening of December 9th. Tired after a daylong trip, they watched in alarm as the agent from the Hotel Regina trundled their luggage to the water's edge and began lowering it into a small black boat. But if they were nervous about traveling in a gondola to their hotel, their gondolier was downright terrified as he watched Wilna awkwardly clamber into his long, narrow craft. In the dark, with the boat rocking, she managed to put one foot in the water while climbing in, then nearly fell out the other side before dropping heavily into her seat. As the gondola shuddered and settled so deeply into the water that it finally sat only half an inch above the water line, peals of nervous laughter erupted from the giddy travelers, but not from the gondolier.

The Hotel Regina was (and remains) one of the best hotels in the city, sitting at the mouth of the Grand Canal and affording its guests a panoramic view of the lagoon with San Giorgio Maggiore in the distance. The magnificent baroque church of Santa Maria della Salute sits only a few hundred yards away, a dramatic view that Nan sketched from their window. In addition to their usual detailed survey of local paintings—and mosaics—the girls visited the Island of Murano, where Wilna spent hours watching the glass blowers and mosaic artists at work.

After the initial shock of traveling by gondola, the girls decided that they rather liked traditional Venetian transport and opted to terrify several more gondoliers as they made their way around the city. The gondoliers were not the only Venetians impressed by Wilna's size, as it turned out. When Wilna tried to photograph Nan feeding a thousand pigeons in front of St. Mark's Basilica, a flock of nearly one hundred locals gathered around to watch. "You would have thought we were all set up and ready to shoot a picture," Wilna wrote to Dan. Particularly vexing to Wilna, who had always been sensitive to people staring at her in public, was a group of three young men who insisted on standing uncomfortably close to watch this midday spectacle. When one of them had the impudence to come even closer and stand gaping up at her only inches away while his friends laughed at his bravado, Wilna could take it no longer. Summoning her inner Katrinka, she hauled off and slugged him with a mean right hook. When the youth landed—some fifteen feet away—he and his astonished companions beat a hasty retreat and the crowd, laughing and concluding that the performance was over, dispersed.[3]

The Christmas holidays of 1926 were spent in Florence, and while the girls expressed disappointment that there weren't any Christmas trees or Salvation Army Santa Clauses, the Cradle of the Renaissance, with its magnificent sculptures, paintings and architecture, did not fail to enthrall them. Of course, in Italy it was imperative to devote a significant part of each day to eating. If the food in Venice had impressed them—and it had—the food in Florence somehow seemed even better. However, their unrestrained sampling of Italian cuisine, layered as it was upon their previous samplings of French and German cuisine, was producing results that could no longer be ignored. With Nan wailing that she would "bust right out of my clothes before I reach America," and with

Frightening the gondoliers. Wilna and Nan were much amused by the horrified reaction of the Venetian gondoliers when they saw Wilna approaching their boats. Undaunted, and enjoying the joke, Wilna and Nan took photos of each other as they rode through the canals in 1926.

antique hotel room chairs collapsing under Wilna with alarming regularity, the galloping gourmets were forced to confront the situation and take action. Unwilling to actually cut back on lunch and dinner, however, they decided to skip breakfast and go for even longer walks in hopes of burning off some of the calories.[4]

The art and cuisine of Siena were the next delights to be sampled on their descent through the Apennines, followed by a weeklong stay in Rome, where they discovered that their hotel—the Flora—would be the most elegant stopover of the entire trip. It was much too nice, Nan complained, as they were required to dress for dinner every night and endure what they perceived as "high hatting" by a large group of wealthy English gentlemen and their "cold" wives. Feeling awkward and insecure in such surroundings, the two American girls amused each other by impersonating their fellow guests behind their backs.[5]

Even after the glories of the Louvre and the Uffizi, both of the young artists were stunned by the sheer amount of art the city of Rome contained, in particular the massive collections of the Vatican museums. "I feel as though I will do some great things after my visit here," Nan enthusiastically told her father. "This trip has certainly meant a great deal to me and I have gotten just as much out of it as tho I were studying with a teacher."[6]

After a week in Naples, and a side trip to see the ancient frescoes in Pompeii, the travelers had planned on an extended stay in the art colony of Vence, in southern France. But on the day they were to set foot on the French Riviera, Nan penned a quick note to her father from Tunis. For reasons they never explained, they had decided at the last minute to make a quick trip—without benefit of Cook's agents—to North Africa. It was a decision they would regret. Their trip to Tunisia, on seas so rough they spent most of the time in their bunks, took two days. For the first time since they left New York, neither of them had any appetite.

The stressful sea voyage, followed as it was by the next phase of this unplanned adventure—a seven-hundred-mile journey by rail to the colorful oasis town of Biskra on the edge of the Sahara Desert—took its toll on Wilna. She came down with a strep throat and raging fever, followed by a severe gallbladder attack likely brought on by her imprudent diet of the previous two months. Armed with only a bottle of Argyrol antiseptic, laxatives and some rubbing alcohol, Nan did what she could to minister to Wilna's needs, but mostly in vain. After a week of struggling to communicate in French with an Algerian doctor, Nan bundled Wilna onto an overnight train to Algiers, where they boarded a ship to Marseille. With a persistent fever and an inflamed gallbladder, Wilna was unable to leave her bed for weeks. Frustrated by her inability to find a nurse "in the second largest city to Paris," Nan decided they should consider starting for home earlier than planned. Though she still felt the trip to North Africa was worth it—she was thrilled to have drawn sketches of "real" Arabs—she also felt they had "seen all we ever want to of Europe," and looked forward to returning to the States. Reluctantly giving up their plan to visit Vence, the demoralized and exhausted travelers boarded an overnight train to Paris at the end of February to make preparations for the voyage back to America.[7]

Despite the rain, Paris proved therapeutic. Wilna was able to have her gallbladder drained at the American Hospital—for free—thanks to one of their expatriate friends who worked there. On a penitential diet of potatoes and prunes and with Nan's constant supervision, Wilna slowly recovered her strength. As they packed for the trip home, Nan reveled in the education she had received and looked forward to making use of all she had learned: "I know my painting when I get home and start in to work, for the Woodstock Gallery exhibition, will show a big improvement after seeing all the fine art of Europe. I am very anxious to get busy at it again."[8]

CHAPTER 10

Treasure Farm

*Opposite: Nan
Mason,* View of
Treasure Farm.
*Oil painting. From
the slope of the
hill just above the
farmhouse, Nan
painted this scene
of Treasure Farm
and the surrounding
countryside coming
to life in the spring.
In those days it was
possible to see all the
way down into the
valley where their
artist friend Dorothy
Varian lived along
Wittenberg Road.*

Within a month of their return to Bearsville in April 1927, Wilna and Nan finalized their purchase of Treasure Farm and an adjoining nine acres on Cooper Lake Road. Wilna purchased yet another ten and a half acres on her own. With their real estate holdings increased by more than forty-seven acres, and in anticipation of moving to the new farm, the girls celebrated by adding another cow to their stable of farm animals. "Daisy" and her twenty quarts of milk a day significantly enhanced the quantities of dairy products they could offer their customers. She also significantly added to the daily chores of the two farm girls.

Before they could actually occupy their new "farm on the hill," and hang the antique bell Wilna had purchased in Florence on the front door of the old house, much work had to be done. The eighteenth-century structure needed a bathroom, a furnace, and a new floor and coal stove in the kitchen. In the vintage kitchen, where the low ceiling with exposed beams constituted a considerable hazard to Wilna's head, workmen performed architectural surgery and cut away enough of each old beam to allow Wilna to pass through the room without mishap.[1]

While they were at it, the girls decided to add on a new room. Two local men, Ishmael Rose, a builder and close neighbor whom the girls had befriended, and Walter Shultis, a stonemason also known for his skill as a fiddler, took on the job of expanding the living space of the old farmhouse. Their first task, digging a footer for the foundation, was hard work and the men became thirsty in the hot sun. Venturing into the kitchen while Wilna was out picking up a visitor at the West Hurley train station, they sought out the jug of applejack she was known to keep stashed under the sink. By the time Wilna returned with her guest, her not-so-secret stash had been somewhat diminished and the jug topped up with ordinary tea. It did not take long for Wilna to discover the substitution. Back at his work and feeling mellow, Shultis suddenly found himself airborne, courtesy of Wilna Hervey. Storming out the door and reaching down into the ditch, she grabbed the suspected culprit by the straps of his overalls and lifted him bodily up onto the dirt pile so she could

The old farmhouse at Treasure Farm. When Wilna and Nan first discovered the "farm on the hill," the two-hundred-year-old house had hardly been changed since it was built in the early eighteenth century. It was even reputed to be haunted. These photos were sent to to Dan Mason so he could see the property they wanted to buy.

confront him face-to-face about his dastardly deed. All was soon forgiven, however, and the story was often told with amusement in the years that followed.[2]

One expense the girls did not have right away at Treasure Farm was the wiring of the house for electricity, as the lines had not yet made their way up the sparsely populated road to Cooper Lake. However, electric lines were now being run up the road from Bearsville to Shady, so in addition to all the work being done on their farmhouse, the girls decided to have electricity installed in their studio cottages that spring.

In addition to the daily care of their chickens, ducks, geese, horses and cows, and the milk runs to sell their dairy products, there was plowing and planting to be done in the spring of 1927, on both the lower and upper farms. Both girls took to the fieldwork with enthusiasm, a fact that alarmed Nan's father. "I think that driving that team over the fields is rather strenuous for you or Nannie," he wrote Wilna. Anticipating her response, he added, "No matter how much you enjoy it. It is man's work . . . "[3] But if the mere thought of such grueling labor wearied the seventy-four-year-old actor, his daughters, at twenty-nine and thirty-one, continued to be invigorated by the fact that their dreams were coming true all around them. Wilna, despite a bout of kidney problems and an episode of chickenpox during the summer, was undaunted by the heavy physical demands of her new life, even climbing trees to pick fruit when the need arose. Later that year, when the Woodstock photographer Alfred Cohn made his splendid portrait of the two young artists, both appeared radiant with health and happiness.

Frustrated to be so far away from the girls as they took possession of the new farm that was intended to be a home for all three of them, and realizing that they were not likely to burden themselves with some of the more mundane details that needed attention, Dan Mason wrote letter after letter filled with practical instructions and advice. "Have the house and barns insured right away before the workmen begin," he urged Wilna in May. He fumed over their immediate acceptance of the high price quoted by the electrician wiring the studios, and reminded them to tell the new tenants that they would have to pay for their own electricity and phone.[4]

In September, after a trip to Syracuse to see his brother, Dan paid a visit to Wilna and Nan to check on their progress and deliver more advice. Before heading back to California, Dan stopped by the bungalow in Audubon, Pennsylvania, and put the house on the market. He shipped all his furniture to Bearsville in preparation for his eventual move there. But he continued to put off making any actual retirement plans, insisting to the girls, even as they pleaded with him to leave Hollywood permanently, that he wanted to make one or two more pictures and increase the legacy he was putting aside for his "Nannie." Much as he longed to enjoy their company, help out on the farm and even relax in the country air, he wanted Nan to be as well off as possible when he was gone and not become dependent on Wilna's fortune. The excellent money he got for his movie work was the means to that end. Dipping into his savings to help pay for Nan's share of the new furnace at Treasure Farm reinforced his conviction that he needed to continue working.[5]

Left: Winter farm chores. Wilna and Nan feed their livestock during one of the rare winters they remained on the farm in Bearsville. They quickly discovered that their romantic notions of evenings in front of a log fire after a brisk day of farm work did not match the harsh realities of tending to farm animals in the winter.

Right: Sleigh Belles. Wilna and Nan, with their dog Teddy (at their feet) in a sleigh pulled by their horse Queenie, at the Jack Horner Tea Room in Woodstock. Molly Pollock, who was visiting, sits on an auxiliary sled behind them, an arrangement reminiscent of the open-air platform that was often pulled behind the Toonerville Trolley.

Mindful of Dan Mason's frequent exhortations to "lift up your thoughts," if they were to maintain good health, both girls continued to pursue their artistic dreams in between their daily farm chores. With a renewed enthusiasm born of her European art tour, Nan devoted herself to painting with the same fervor she invested in gardening, making cheese or baking custard pies. Her work was rapidly improving, a fact not lost on Wilna, who presented her partner with a splendid new canvas for her birthday in July. For her first "real" canvas, Nan chose a view of the old barns on the property. When the work was shown at the third Woodstock art exhibition that summer, *Our Barns* received positive comment in the local press.[6]

While Nan painted their barns, Wilna went on a treasure hunt, exploring the old legend that gave the farm its name. It was said that, during the Revolution, a family

The "lower farm" in the winter of 1927/28. The original Hervey–Mason homestead was complete with barn, chicken coop and storage sheds by the time the girls began relocating up the hill to Treasure Farm. This shot was taken from one of the fields that they plowed and planted in the summer.

fleeing the burning of Kingston had taken refuge in the Bearsville farmhouse and buried a gold pitcher and a silver box for safekeeping along the bluestone path that led to their door. However, in 1927 no such path was to be seen. On a hunch, Wilna poked around with a rod and found the old flagstones, now buried six inches down under a century and a half of accumulated dirt. Then she started digging. She would later claim to have found a silver snuffbox, engraved with a Masonic emblem, and a silver spoon. However, another version of this story suggests that it was the workmen who dug the foundation for the new room who actually found the snuffbox and spoon, along with a pair of hand-made scissors. No golden pitcher has ever been discovered.[7]

Even before they officially moved to Treasure Farm, the collection of livestock Wilna and Nan had assembled attracted attention. Late in 1927 a newly arrived artist and

▲ 73 ▲

Caroline Speare Rohland, Wilna and Nan in Bearsville. *Standing in the snow at the "lower farm," the girls take a break from their chores to pose for a quick photo with Teddy, one of the two collies they acquired in Audubon. In the background on the left can be seen their chicken coop, later used as a studio. The barn stands to the right.*

novice filmmaker, Gustave Schrader, asked the girls if he could pay them a visit to shoot some footage of their "stock farm" with his movie camera. Not having been in front of a camera in nearly six years, the erstwhile actresses enthusiastically agreed to Schrader's request, although the footage they provided him was not exactly the portrait of bucolic life that he was after. Co-starring with their animals, Wilna and Nan put on a show for Schrader. Wilna demonstrated a milking technique that shot the liquid directly into the cat's mouth, while Nan put one of the collies through his paces. Their horse, not to be outdone, rolled on the ground like a dog. Other animals, "apparently well trained for the cinema," according to an eyewitness, performed as well. For a finale, the girls did a dance routine that ended with them freezing in a pose as the scene faded to black. Combined with other footage he had shot in the community, Schrader showed his film to audiences all over Woodstock early in 1928. Anyone in the valley who had not yet met Wilna and Nan certainly knew who they were now.[8]

Nan Mason, Home Grown Fruit. *Oil painting. Both Wilna and Nan thought nothing of climbing trees to pick the best fruit. Beyond the obvious advantage of growing their own food, another benefit for the girls was the endless supply of new material for impromptu still life studies. Nan's interest in the work of the French Post-Impressionist painter Paul Cézanne can be detected in this composition.*

While traveling in Europe, the girls had read about heavy snowfalls in the Woodstock area. They were sorry to have missed these and pledged to stay in Bearsville through the next winter and "rough it."[9] Nan looked forward to painting the landscape of Treasure Farm covered in snow. Mother Nature did not disappoint. There were ample opportunities during their first winter in the Catskills for Wilna and Nan to get snowed in and warm themselves before log fires after trudging through snowdrifts to complete their rounds of the barns. Rather than shovel out the long driveway, the girls hitched their horse, Queenie, to an old sleigh, bundled themselves in furs, and glided over the snowy roads to one of their favorite haunts to eat, drink and sing with the other hardy souls who had ventured out in search of winter camaraderie.

In the midst of moving to their new home, in early April 1928, Nan suddenly needed surgery for an undisclosed ailment. Whatever the malady was, the operation was serious enough to keep Nan in the hospital for two weeks and require several weeks of recuperation after her return to Bearsville. In a rare reversal of roles, Wilna had to tend to Nan, and take over all of Nan's duties around the house and the farm. While recovering, Nan made good use of the fact that she was not supposed to move by posing for the sculptor Paul Fiene, who added her portrait to his ongoing studies of Woodstock artists. His *Bust of Nan Mason* would debut the following summer.[10]

By June 1928 Nan had fully recovered and had even entered another painting in the Woodstock Artists Association's first exhibition of the season. With all the house renovations finished, and all furnishings and animals moved to Treasure Farm, Wilna and Nan decided they had much to celebrate. Following the June 22nd opening of the Association's show featuring Nan's latest work, they invited their favorite people back to Treasure Farm

An evening with the Speichers and the Rosens. Throughout the thirties and forties, Wilna and Nan's closest friends in Woodstock were Eugene and Elsie Speicher and Charles and Jean Rosen. The three couples were frequently together for dinner, drinks, card games or just socializing. Charles Rosen is partly hidden by Elsie Speicher in this photo taken by his wife.

Henry Lee McFee, Eugene Speicher and Charles Rosen. As both friend and mentor, each of these prominent Woodstock artists played a significant role in the lives and careers of Wilna and Nan. McFee encouraged Wilna's dramatic midlife shift to the naïve style for which she became famous. Rosen's emphasis on solid geometry can be seen as an influence in Nan's early art. Speicher, whom Wilna first met in 1918, became a lifelong friend who provided both of the girls with much encouragement and moral support.

for an official housewarming party. After dinner, the eighteen guests retired to the parlor where an abundance of applejack (the "official" Woodstock drink during prohibition) fueled high spirits. In the absence of electricity, kerosene lamps were used to illuminate the evening's musical entertainment. Nan's rendering of the music hall chestnut "Poor John," while dressed in one of her mother's old gowns, was the hit of the evening.[11] This inaugural party was such a success that they threw an even larger one a month later. Unable to attend the second party, in part because they were still hung over from another recent outing, Henry Lee and Aileen McFee later reported to the girls that all their friends said the party had been a "knock out."[12] Over the next fifty years, in a community known for its parties, the Big Girls' gatherings were to become the stuff of legend.

Even when they weren't throwing big parties, Wilna and Nan were seldom without visitors or guests at Treasure Farm. At one point, while their own house in Rock City was being renovated, Eugene and Elsie Speicher made themselves at home in the girls' old farmhouse on the hill for the duration. Speicher made a drawing of the panoramic vista as seen from the slope above the house, choosing almost the same vantage point that Nan had favored in her own landscape painting of their view. During one of his frequent visits to Treasure Farm, Charles Rosen took advantage of the opportunity to draw the weathered barns framed by old apple trees and made a gift of the sketch to Nan and Wilna. The painter Dorothy Varian recalled that any time Wilna spotted her outside her cottage—a quarter of a mile down the hill on the Wittenberg Road—she would hear Wilna's voice on the wind, shouting that she should "come on up" for coffee or a drink. The sound of tires on the long red gravel driveway, announcing the arrival of unexpected visitors, was part of the Treasure Farm routine, encouraged by the enthusiastic responses such impromptu visits elicited. "Even when I went to see them without calling first," one old friend remembered, "they acted like they had just been sitting there waiting for me to show up."[13]

▲ ▲ ▲

Dan Mason's final film, *Hop Off*, was released in July 1928, and while he continued to seek new parts his career was in fact over. "I must confess I am not feeing as good as I have been," he wrote to the girls in mid-October. "Have had a fever and chills all through my body. . . . I went to my bed. It was the only place I could get warm."[14] Worried about his welfare, Nan and Wilna decided to go to California. In late October, the newly installed owners of Treasure Farm once again found temporary quarters for all their animals and—for the second time in three years—abandoned Bearsville as the cold weather set in.

The Hollywood that Wilna Hervey and Nan Mason visited that fall was a different place from the one they had left only four years earlier. All of the studios and

Eugene Speicher, Drawing of Our Farm *(Wilna Hervey and Nan Mason's Bearsville Home). Speicher drew this panoramic scene from a vantage point similar to the one Nan had chosen years earlier for her painting of the farm. Looking down from the hillside above the house, Speicher's work shows the impressive view that Wilna and Nan enjoyed from their home. The drawing is inscribed, "To Willie with love from Gene."*

Charles Rosen, Barns and Apple Tree. *A portrait of the barns at Treasure Farm. Rosen gave Nan this conté crayon drawing of the barns at Treasure Farm for her birthday in 1933. Typical of Rosen's kindness and sensitivity toward his friends, he inscribed it, "Happy Birthday to Nan from Charlie." Then, not wanting Wilna to feel left out, he added, parenthetically, "and Willie too!"*

many of the theaters were installing equipment to accommodate the new "talkies." Just who would benefit from the dramatic change and who might be destroyed by the new technology was a discussion heard in many quarters. What the veteran character actor Dan Mason could or would do was another subject much debated among the three people to whom it mattered most. Though he suspected sound movies were just a passing fad, Dan had already done a successful voice test and lined up a speaking part in a new film. But Dan was definitely not well. The seventy-five-year-old was burdened not only by fatigue and other vague discomforts but also by a respiratory ailment that proved impossible to shake. He was in no condition to take on any kind of new role, no matter how minor. Unknown to Dan, who avoided doctors on the grounds that they did more harm than good and were in any case much too expensive, he was suffering from chronic kidney disease and had recently contracted tuberculosis.[15]

As the holidays approached, Dan became so ill that his daughters insisted on taking him back east for an extended stay with his brother in Syracuse. They hoped a long vacation would help him regain his strength. But his health continued to fail and by spring, still unseen by a doctor, Dan was barely able to function on his own. Alarmed by his decline, Nan drove to Syracuse and brought her father back to Bearsville to care for him personally.

Dan would never live at Treasure Farm as he had hoped and, ironically, he wasn't able to die there either. With the stairs in the old farmhouse proving an insurmountable obstacle, Nan was forced to make her enfeebled father comfortable in one of the little studio cottages along the state road. The local press, unaware of the actual situation, cheerfully reported that the noted actor would spend the summer in Bearsville. But a month later Dan was dead. By the time he finally consented to be seen by a doctor, there was nothing the doctor could do.

Dan Mason, veteran star of stage and screen, actor, singer, dancer and writer, the "tangled Teutonic talker" of vaudeville fame, the irascible Skipper of the Toonerville Trolley, died in the early hours of July 6th, 1929, his beloved daughters at his side. Just before he died, Dan made his girls promise that they would never let their friendship fade. They assured him they would not. He asked Wilna to promise that she would forever take care of his "Nannie." Echoing the phrase Dan always used when signing his letters, Wilna promised, "with all my heart."[16]

Motivated by distrust of his son, Harry, Dan Mason left his entire estate to Nan. In addition to his savings, Nan inherited the little house in Los Angeles; renting it would provide her with some much-needed income for years. Dan had also recently sold the bungalow in Audubon, and the payments on the mortgage her father had made would now come directly to Nan.[17] While these new sources of income more than replaced Dan's monthly support for Nan's lifestyle, nothing could replace the constant loving encouragement of the only parent either one of them had left, or the sound, if occasionally prickly, advice he had so freely provided. Dan Mason would be sorely missed.

In September, two and half months after Dan Mason's death, the New York Stock Exchange began to falter, and in late October came the infamous stock market crash that

Dan Mason. Although in costume and makeup as Pop Tuttle, Nan's father displays an expression of skeptical bemusement that transcended his acting and was a familiar sight to his girls. His down-to-earth approach to life served as a counterpoint to Wilna and Nan's mercurial tendencies.

signaled the beginning of the Great Depression. Two weeks before the financial panic began to sweep the country, Wilna added another thirteen acres to her real estate holdings in Bearsville.[18] She and Nan now held more than eighty acres, much of it mortgaged. Several of their parcels—as Nan's father had strenuously pointed out on more than one occasion—did nothing more than tie up money, earn no income and cost them cash in the form of taxes. In addition to mortgages, taxes and insurance on the farm, there were feed and veterinary bills stemming from the need to care for their many animals. There were bills from carpenters and plumbers and well-diggers. While both Wilna and Nan had significant financial resources, the inherited wealth that made both girls feel so secure faced a more uncertain future than they knew. But this fact was not so apparent in late 1929 and early 1930. With President Hoover, his Secretary of the Treasury, Andrew Mellon, and the governor of New York, Franklin Roosevelt, all dismissing worries and exuding confidence in the strength of the economy, it was easy to remain optimistic.[19]

Thus it wasn't the cold wind of economic change, but the frost and snow flurries heralding another Woodstock winter that commanded the attention of the two wealthiest girls in Bearsville in the late fall of 1929. Not particularly interested in a repeat of their frozen adventures of previous winters, Wilna and Nan once again closed up their house, boarded all the animals with the neighbors and headed to California. During their 1922 visit to Wilna's brother, Thomas Cator, both of the young artists had been impressed with the beauty of Carmel-by-the-Sea and enjoyed the atmosphere of the burgeoning art colony there. Wilna had even bought property in Carmel and promised to return. They now decided to spend the winter painting in the picturesque little village overlooking the ocean.

CHAPTER 11

"You Gals Certainly Are Fortunate"

*Opposite: Wilna
Hervey playing
softball in Carmel-
by-the-Sea. Wilna's
enthusiasm and
strength made her
a star player on her
Carmel softball
team. Pity the poor
outfielders. As with
her approach to
kicking a football,
Wilna always
attempted to bat the
softball "to hell and
gone!"*

If Wilna and Nan didn't immediately experience the economic woes of the deepening Depression, many of their friends in Woodstock did. By the summer of 1930 many of the local artists were already out of money and some couldn't even buy groceries. In fact, the situation for some of the artists in Woodstock was so bleak that Juliana Force, the director of the Whitney Museum in Manhattan and a friend to many of the Woodstock painters, made special trips to Woodstock to visit artists she knew and buy their works in the hope of keeping them afloat. She went so far on one occasion as to crawl through the window of an artist's shack on the Maverick, take a painting she liked, and leave behind a note with three hundred dollars.[1]

While not unaware of the plight of several of their friends, Wilna and Nan nevertheless remained largely oblivious to the realities of what was happening around them. The one and only precaution they took as economic conditions worsened was to make sure that all of their Bearsville properties were owned by both of them as "joint tenants." That way, if one of them died, the survivor would inherit everything and not have to fend off relatives making claims on the estate. Otherwise, seemingly unconcerned by the darkening economic conditions and confident that their resources were inexhaustible, they continued to spend money as though nothing had changed. As they headed to California, they often stopped to buy and send gifts to several people back in Woodstock, but did so frivolously and with no apparent intent to shore up the situation of those in need.[2]

For the four years from 1929 to 1933 Wilna and Nan alternated between the two art colonies three thousand miles apart. With Nan doing most of the driving and Wilna riding shotgun (literally—she was afraid of Gypsies), they piloted Wilna's big new Durant out to Carmel in the fall and back to Woodstock the following spring. In Carmel, as in Woodstock, they cultivated friendships among the resident artists and showed their works in local exhibitions. Each of them occasionally sold a few pieces. The multicultural community of Monterey County provided Wilna with a variety of ethnic types for her

▲ 80 ▲

Nan Mason, Wilna Hervey on the Beach at Carmel-by-the-Sea. *As with her talents for drawing and painting, Nan's abilities as a photographer asserted themselves early on. The poetic shapes of the old native pines around Carmel were much appreciated by both artists.*

portrait studies. Both artists painted local attractions that appealed to them, such as the ocean piers where they not only fished alongside the locals but sat down to sketch as well. They took long walks along the beach, taking snapshots and looking for vignettes to draw or paint. If anything, their social lives in Carmel were even richer than in Woodstock. In addition to joining local softball teams, they lent their dramatic and comedic talents to the Carmel Community Players, appearing in plays and devising vaudeville routines.[3]

One of the closest friends they acquired in Carmel was the photographer Edward Weston, who maintained a studio on Wildcat Hill, overlooking the coast just south of the village. Weston wrote of one particularly memorable party attended by the two girls from Woodstock:

Sunday night we held a party to be remembered, a rare gathering which brought together congenial persons who like to play, be gay; not one of them was a false note, each contributing to the fun, and spontaneously. Came: Fernando Felix who plays the guitar and sings—

Wilna Hervey, Othia *and* Monteyo. *The only extant works done by Wilna during her several seasons in Carmel, these portraits reflect her longstanding interest in ethnic portraiture and the ongoing influence of Winold Reiss. Wilna gave these drawings to her Bearsville neighbors, the artists Theodore M. Wassmer and his wife, Judy Farnsworth Lund.*

> Mexican songs of course—Nacho Bravo, who dances the Rhumba . . . Wilna Hervey and Nan Mason, who played and sang in their delightful way; and then the group who have been gathering lately for dancing and vino. . . . We had plenty of good vino, white and red, Fernando's singing was memorable, Xenia sang in Russian, Sonya in Spanish and Polish, I improvised, danced a Kreutzberg, and a "Spring" number, also I danced with Wilna who is almost a foot taller than I am, and must weigh 350! It was a party without one dull moment . . .[4]

Small wonder Wilna was able to photograph Nan so drunk that the resultant snapshot just had to be sent to the McFees for their amusement. Wilna's old friend Molly Pollock laughed at the stories of their adventures in Carmel: "Oh, you gals certainly are fortunate in being [able] to live as you do."[5]

During the four years that Wilna and Nan divided their time between the two art colonies, Wilna bought three more properties in Bearsville and, together with Nan, purchased four more near Carmel, in the hills south of town. Their first joint acquisition

Nan Mason, View of Bearsville. *This autumn scene is one of only two of Nan's large landscapes in oils that can be located today. The view shows the extent to which the hills around Woodstock were still devoid of trees in those days. It also shows the influence of both of Nan's mentors, George Bellows (color) and Charles Rosen (solid geometry). The even, chisel-like brush strokes call to mind the work of Cézanne.*

in California was a parcel in an exclusive community just being developed, purchased shortly after their arrival in the fall of 1929. Clearly intending to make Carmel a permanent second home where she could paint and enjoy the company of her brother and his family, Wilna began building a house on this prime lot overlooking the ocean. Leery of the big storms that sometimes roared in from the Pacific, Wilna, who was terrified of lightning and ran shrieking for the safety of the nearest closet at the first rumble of thunder, included a cyclone cellar in the architectural plans. "A refuge from movie directors," Nan joked to a reporter. "We're going to do nothing but paint." Wilna justified this considerable expense with the rationale that when they were not in town they could rent the house just as they often tried to do with their home in Bearsville during the winter. As the other parcels they bought already had homes on them (in two instances they took over the mortgages from widows), it was their intention to rent these for income as well. Through all of these purchases, Wilna blithely ignored the fact that only two years earlier, when she was preoccupied with preparing Treasure Farm for occupancy, she had allowed her previously purchased properties in Carmel to be sold for taxes, a lapse of judgment that had made Nan's father nearly apoplectic.[6]

In the spring of 1931 Wilna and Nan were so reluctant to leave Carmel that they didn't return to Treasure Farm until June, too late for any serious plowing and planting and a clear indication that the whole idea of living off the soil had withered on the vine. In fact, as Wilna had told a reporter in Carmel, she envisioned her farm in Bears-ville "dotted with artist's studios" rather than crops.[7] As the yearly boarding of the live-stock with neighbors for seven months became an expensive logistical nightmare—and a nuisance for all concerned—the farm animals were slowly phased out and sold. Nan's insistence to a Carmel reporter that all they intended to do was paint was a dictum that applied equally to their Woodstock lives. They would soon lease part of Treasure Farm to a local farmer.

▲ ▲ ▲

In terms of output and recognition, the early years of the Great Depression, when she and Wilna were shuttling back and forth between Woodstock and Carmel, were among Nan Mason's best years as an artist. Only five years after the 1922 sketch in Carmel that launched her career in art, and only three years after beginning formal training with George Bellows, Nan was a member of the Woodstock Artists Association regularly exhibiting her own work.[8] While she displayed a number of still life paintings and at least one print in the late twenties and early thirties, it was her landscapes—done on both coasts—for which she became well known and received critical acclaim. A panoramic view of a ranch in California received favorable comment when it was exhibited in the third Woodstock show of 1931, and her seascape *Monterey Fishing Boats* excited attention at the fourth show a month later. During the early winter of 1931, when the girls had remained in Bearsville for a few extra months, Nan painted a snowy Woodstock farm

Nan Mason, Tug Boats, Kingston, N.Y. *Print. Charles Rosen's influence on Nan's style can be seen in this view of the tugboats at Rondout, near Kingston, the locale of some of Rosen's iconic paintings. Nan would revisit Rondout thirty years later, this time with a camera instead of a sketchbook.*

scene. This work, which she called *February*, was shown in the Salons of America exhibition at the Anderson Galleries in New York City the following year. *February* was also chosen to be part of an exhibition sponsored by the College Art Association that traveled all over the United States. Included in this show were three hundred and seventy-nine works by some four dozen artists, many of whom, like Eugenie McEvoy, Florence Cramer and Ernest Fiene, were Nan's Woodstock friends.[9]

The fall and early winter of 1932 were especially gratifying professionally for Nan. In September 1932 another of her snowscapes, *The Highwoods*—a view of a quaint frame church in nearby Saugerties—went on display in a show at the Midtown Gallery in Manhattan. The *New York Sun* published a photo of Nan's work as an illustration for its report on the opening of the exhibition. A month later Nan painted an autumn view of Bearsville. Heralding the arrival of Wilna and Nan in Carmel in the late fall of 1932, the local press noted, "Miss Mason has achieved a national name for her landscape work." In December one of Nan's drawings on exhibit at the Carmel Art Association, of which she (but not Wilna) had become a member, was mentioned in the local paper there.[10]

By the early spring of 1933 Wilna and Nan had comfortably established themselves as part of the Carmel art community. They had paid off the mortgage on their San Remo property with its splendid new house, and had placed enough of their works in local

The home of Ruth Hart Eddy on Anna Maria Island. Situated on Beach Avenue close to the water, Miss Eddy's opulent Mediterranean-style villa featured a red tiled roof, wrought iron gates, rounded doors and lush landscaping. A visit to this home in 1934, at the invitation of Ruth Eddy and her companion, Alice Gilman, was Wilna and Nan's first exposure to Florida's mild winter weather and inspired their decision to make the island paradise their seasonal retreat.[1]

Ruth Hart Eddy in 1923. Since Miss Eddy ordered all photographs of herself to be destroyed upon her death, only this image from her U.S. passport application survives. She was thirty-eight years old at the time. Wilna and Nan's friendship with this wealthy, wise and compassionate woman was one of the most important of their lives.

shows that Henry Lee McFee sent them a letter of congratulations: "[I]t is often slow in getting started but once it starts it is like a snow ball going down hill," he assured them. "Keep up the good work."[11] Yet this would turn out to be their last season in Carmel. In the autumn of 1933, after a very successful summer in Woodstock, where they both showed works they had just produced in California, they remained at Treasure Farm instead of making their annual trek to Carmel. They would never return to Carmel again, neither to live in the newly completed house overlooking the Pacific, nor to paint in the pine-covered hills that Wilna loved so much. Instead, after spending most of the winter in Bearsville, they headed south in March 1934, eager to accept the invitation of a new friend, Ruth Hart Eddy, to visit at her vacation home in Florida.

Ruth Hart Eddy, then a resident of Troy, New York, was an extremely wealthy woman. She had inherited the fortune made by her grandfather, who invented the ink used by the federal government to print currency. With her widowed mother, Miss Eddy had founded the James A. Eddy Memorial Foundation at the Samaritan Hospital in Troy to care for the elderly. She ran the foundation, made herself an expert on hospitals, and along the way employed an assistant, Alice Gilman, who became her life companion as well. In 1928 Ruth Eddy built a sprawling Mediterranean-style home on Anna Maria Island, off the west coast of Florida. There, she and Alice Gilman would arrive in a chauffeur-driven Cadillac each winter to spend six months, attended to by a staff of servants.[12] It was to this sumptuous home on Beach Avenue, overlooking the Gulf of Mexico, that Wilna and Nan headed in the spring of 1934.

Just how or when the girls from Bearsville met the Misses Eddy and Gilman is uncertain. A sophisticated collector of art and antiques, Ruth Eddy was a friend of Eugene Speicher, whom she had commissioned to paint her mother's portrait. It is likely that the Speichers—who had already introduced Wilna and Nan to several of their influential friends, such as Juliana Force—made the connection to Eddy and Gilman. In any

Below: Paul Juley, Wilna Hervey, Woodstock, 1934. *A pensive and wary Wilna sits beneath Nan's painting* February *at Treasure Farm in 1934. The Juleys made no attempt to show Wilna at work as an artist, a lapse that apparently upset her.*

Above: Paul Juley, Nan Mason at Work in Her Studio, Woodstock, 1934. *This photo, taken at Treasure Farm, shows Nan at her easel, her painting of the High Woods Church before her and the autumn landscape of 1932 leaning against the wall. The Juleys used Nan's paintings as props to emphasize her reputation as an emerging landscape artist.*

case, the two couples hit it off immediately and were soon corresponding and visiting. Wilna and Nan stayed only a month with their new acquaintances on this first visit, marveling at the wonderful weather, fishing off the piers and deluging their friends back in Woodstock with gifts of grapefruit. By the time they packed up the car for the trip back home, they had decided that in the future Florida would be a far better place for them to spend the winter than California. The girls' acquaintanceship with Ruth Eddy and Alice Gilman would blossom into a close lifelong friendship, one that would ultimately have profound and unexpected consequences for Wilna and Nan.

▲ ▲ ▲

When the fine art photographers Peter Juley and his son Paul arrived in Woodstock in 1934 to document the art colony, it was Nan Mason, and her reputation as a noted landscape painter, that attracted their visit to Treasure Farm. As it turned out, the Juleys

Nan and Wilna at Treasure Farm in the late thirties. Nan reads while Wilna draws in these two photos they took of each other relaxing at the farmhouse during the Christmas holidays. Notes on the back of the photos indicate that the little painting seen just above Wilna's head was a recent gift from the Woodstock artist Ethel Magafan and that the Christmas tree was made by Fritzi Striebel.[2]

photographed Wilna and Nan at a turning point in their professional lives. Three of Nan's landscapes—which the photographers seem to have used as props—can be seen in several photos, but their very presence in the studio may have been a source of frustration for Nan. All three pieces, painted years before, had been included in noteworthy exhibitions and received critical acclaim. None had sold, however, perhaps due to the deepening Depression, and by 1934 Nan was re-evaluating the amount of time, energy and cash she was putting into large-scale landscape painting in oils. But the lack of sales may not be the main reason Nan began to back away from her successful work. Many artists, after all, failed to sell work during the Depression and yet kept painting, and Nan was prone to chronic optimism.

It is possible that Wilna had something to do with Nan's change of direction, albeit unwittingly. Paul Juley photographed Nan standing proudly at her easel, and the only paintings seen in all the shots they took that day are Nan's. Wilna is not portrayed as an artist in any way, nor is any of her work to be seen. One photo shows Wilna eyeing the camera warily and uncomfortably. It is a surprising image given Wilna's love of being photographed and her reputation for joyous hospitality, even to those who dropped in unexpectedly. Wilna's ambivalent mood as she sat beneath Nan's *February* may reflect the fact that the Juleys did not focus attention on her as they did with Nan, and had no reason to. Unlike her partner, Wilna had exhibited only a couple of new pieces with the Woodstock Artists Association in the previous several years, gotten little notice, and had shown nothing in Manhattan.[13]

It is not impossible that Wilna's dissatisfaction with her lackluster artistic efforts at this juncture inspired Nan's decision to wind down her own efforts. While Wilna had always expressed delight in Nan's rapid development as an artist, to Nan and to all their friends, it is also true that her partner's swift success and recognition had the effect of coaxing the spotlight away from Wilna, who was used to being the celebrity partner. Sensitive to Wilna's emotional state, and throughout her life inclined to make a priority of Wilna's happiness and comfort, Nan may have decided that maintaining the "harmony between you," in the words of her father, required that she not succeed at the expense of Wilna's self-esteem. Whatever the reason, whether a victim of the economic Depression or Wilna's depression, Nan's landscape painting came to an end. The inclusion of *February* in an exhibition in Woodstock in the summer of 1935 would mark the end of the series of landscapes that Nan had shown on a yearly basis since 1928. Though she would continue to grow artistically, and would develop skills in several other genres in the years ahead, Nan would never return to the work that had brought her national attention. Ironically, as the Juleys documented the rising young landscape painter Nan Mason, they actually recorded the end of her serious efforts in that genre.

Drifting in the artistic doldrums and unhappy about it, Wilna was about to be pointed in a whole new artistic direction by her close friend and occasional drinking buddy Henry Lee McFee. A radical whose own work had once shocked the more conservative artists in Woodstock, McFee urged Wilna to step out of the shadow of Winold Reiss and adopt her own style, one that reflected her unique personality. It would take a few years for the seeds of this idea to germinate, but what eventually emerged was a whimsical, childlike style that Wilna would affect for the rest of her career and for which she would be best known.[14]

The visit of Peter and Paul Juley to Treasure Farm coincided with the long-delayed realization on the part of the farm's two owners that their finances were in serious trouble. Maintaining their house cost money, in terms of both taxes and upkeep. There were significant bills for work done on the farmhouse and the studio cottages in June and August 1934, and a hefty tax bill for the farm would follow in December. Yet, as rents declined nationwide, the bicoastal landladies found the income from their several properties diminishing accordingly. While it is unknown how Nan's inheritance was invested, it cannot have remained unscathed by the worsening Depression. The amount of Wilna's monthly checks declined as the Hervey Post Trust fought to stay afloat amidst the collapse of many of its investments. In the summer of 1934, when the

Nan with Henry Lee and Aileen McFee on an unidentified Florida beach. This winter visit with their friends was one of the last times Wilna and Nan would see the couple together. Less than a year later, Aileen McFee would have a heart attack and her husband would abandon her to run off with her niece, never to see Woodstock again.

Trust was forced to sell a sizeable chunk of its real estate holdings in New Jersey to raise needed cash, Wilna finally realized that her financial security was not ensured after all. She confided to one of her friends in Woodstock that her situation was becoming worrisome.[15]

In the face of growing economic uncertainty, Dan Mason would have counseled discretion, and advised his girls to embrace austerity measures until they could see their way clear to some certainty and security. But Dan and his logical financial advice—sometimes sketched out in detailed charts accounting for every last cent—were gone now, leaving his daughter and her mercurial partner to follow their bliss.

Therefore, unpaid invoices and tax bills aside, as fall arrived and winter weather threatened to engulf Woodstock once again, Wilna and Nan hastened to Florida, eager to bask in the sun and see their new friends on Anna Maria Island. With the help of Ruth Eddy, they managed to find a tiny cottage at a rock-bottom rate. Once encamped, they drove across the state to see the McFees, who were spending the winter in St. Augustine. Afterward they sent Henry Lee amusing photos that showed just how drunk he had gotten during their visit. They scoured the beaches of Anna Maria for seashells, tucked little poems into each one, packed them into a handcrafted, hand-painted box, and sent them to Caroline Rohland, who declared herself "shell shocked." And they deluged Eugene and Elsie Speicher with so many crates of fruit that Gene Speicher suggested they were exhausting the nation's supply. "All that fruit! . . . Elsie and I are so healthy from drinking fruit juice I think we will try for the most healthy boy and girl, Mr. and Mrs. America," he assured them. That Wilna and Nan could ill afford this idyllic winter vacation was given no more thought than how the waves washed away their footprints on the beach.[16]

Stage, Screen and Radio

When Wilna Hervey and Nan Mason returned to Bearsville from Florida in April 1935, their financial problems, like the ever-present mice in the barn, were there waiting for them. As they took up their usual summer routine of gardening and painting, Wilna had trouble putting her heart into any of it. Frustrated artistically, done with farming and feeling the economic pinch, the one-time "Katrinka of the Cinema" longed for the days when she could make quick and easy money in the movies. Ignoring the difficulties she had encountered trying to get parts in 1923, Wilna wrote to Frank Capra, now a successful director at Columbia Pictures, and asked his advice. "There is absolutely no reason why there shouldn't be something doing for you in pictures," Capra replied. "I may not have anything for you myself at the moment, but there is plenty going on around here . . . I shall be very happy to see you both." This was all the encouragement Wilna needed. For her part, Nan was more than happy to abandon the farmstead and traverse the continent in pursuit of another of Wilna's dreams. Three weeks later the girls loaded up the car and headed for California. The local paper reported that "both expect to be engaged in making pictures for one of the studios."[1]

For the next eight months, Wilna and Nan lived in Hollywood in the little Spanish-style bungalow on North Stanley Avenue that Nan had inherited from her father. This meant, of course, that the property was not bringing in any rental income during that time. The girls visited Frank Capra, made the rounds of the studios, and took side trips to Sierra Madre and to Mexico. But mostly they waited for the phone to ring or telegrams to arrive. One measure of Wilna's restless frustration with the endless waiting was the orgy of gift-giving she indulged in for weeks on end. Everywhere they went, Wilna saw, and in spite of their limited resources impulsively purchased, gifts to send to friends back in Woodstock. Her favorite friends, Eugene and Elsie Speicher, were singled out for special attention, receiving olives, multiple handkerchiefs, bottles of tequila and Tweed

cologne. The Speichers were well-to-do and in spite of the Depression lived a lifestyle of tuxedos and evening gowns, massages and martinis, and Wilna's relentless largesse apparently made Elsie uncomfortable. When one shower of gifts prompted Elsie to gently scold Wilna for spending scarce money unnecessarily, Wilna reacted like a toddler whose bouquet of wilted dandelions has been rejected. She responded with such a "sad letter" that Elsie felt obliged to quickly apologize: "I know . . . your extravagance only comes from the loveliest of impulses . . . in the meantime, know that Gene and I love you and that is the only reason we take the trouble to scold you." Wilna's response to this billet-doux was another shower of gifts.[2]

As the waiting for callbacks stretched over months, and the offers of parts failed to materialize, Wilna accompanied her gifts with letters bewailing her circumstances, eliciting many sympathetic and encouraging messages in return. "I just think you two girls are so much too good for Hollywood," Louise Lindin (Mrs. Carl Eric Lindin) wrote in March. "But if you need the money I expect that is the surest way to get it." The McFees and the Petershams urged them to return to Woodstock. "It won't be right without you there," Maud Petersham wrote to Wilna in February 1936. "We miss you both, so do not stay away long."[3]

Increasing the girls' frustration, there were some close calls that raised their hopes only to dash them. "Terribly sorry to hear of the missing of the Laurel and Hardy contract," Louise Lindin wrote to them in March. One of Elsie Speicher's letters refers cryptically to the Marx Brothers, raising the possibility that Wilna and Nan were flirting with an appearance in one of their films. In the end, the only movie role that Wilna is known to have landed, after months of waiting, was a brief uncredited appearance in the Three Stooges film *A Pain in the Pullman*.[4] Since the Stooges were working at Columbia

Wilna confronts The Three Stooges. The only movie role Wilna landed in 1936 was an uncredited appearance with The Three Stooges in A Pain in the Pullman. *Awakened from a sound sleep in the middle of the night by Moe, Larry and Curly, Wilna climbs down from her Pullman berth to find out what is going on. Moments later, the Stooges are sent flying through the air on their way to bed, courtesy of Wilna.*

Ready for her close-up. Hat at a jaunty angle, cigarette in hand and stylishly dressed in the latest nineteen-thirties fashions, Wilna is in full movie star mode as she poses for Nan outside their Los Angeles bungalow. She was likely on her way to an interview or audition.

Pictures, it is possible that Frank Capra, besieged by Wilna for several months, brought her to the attention of the writer/director of the Stooges movies, Preston Black.

Anyone who has seen a Three Stooges movie will appreciate the letters of sympathy Wilna received from her friends when work on the film was completed in early May. "So they banged you all up," Elsie Speicher wrote. "You poor kid. I am terribly sorry. Glad you are better." Caroline Rohland urged Wilna to forgo any further activities that might hurt her: "For heaven's sakes don't do any of that rough stuff again. It is just frightful. *Be sure* not to get into anything any *more near like it!*"[5]

In the film, the Stooges, as itinerant entertainers, are traveling by train and intend to sleep overnight in an upper Pullman berth. However, they have difficulties getting into their bunk and one attempt to catapult Larry into bed results in his flying in the wrong direction and landing heavily on the stomach of a sleeping woman (Wilna), who shrieks in alarm. She decides that the only way she will get any sleep is if she helps them get into their berth. She climbs down and proceeds to heave them bodily into bed, one by one like so many sacks of potatoes.

▲ 95 ▲

Wilna being dressed as "Miss Santa Claus." After her limited success in Hollywood, Wilna tried to conquer Broadway in 1939. Aside from a part in a play that quickly folded, the only "role" she landed was Miss Santa Claus, in a one-day gig for a corporate Christmas party. Ironically, this one small job resulted in her photograph appearing in dozens of newspapers across the country.

Wilna's scene in the final release version of the film is tame by Stooge standards. Even so, filming this scene took all day, with repeated takes leaving Wilna exhausted and covered in bruises and abrasions. It was her only role with the Three Stooges. Despite her ordeal, she was not in a position to turn down another role with them. None was offered, however. Wilna's failure to get any further parts with the Stooges, who used a different large actress in their next film, may have been the result of her giving the rowdy comedians a hard time in a way they didn't expect. In a 1948 interview looking back on her experiences in Hollywood, she told the reporter, "There were some words in [the script] that I simply refused to say and they had to be deleted."[6]

Nan seems not to have secured any parts at all, though it is unclear just how serious her intentions were; this trip to Hollywood was really about Wilna. Ultimately frustrated by their failure to break into the movies again, the girls were also disheartened—and further inconvenienced financially—by Wilna's inability to rent her beautiful house in Carmel and their failure to get more than a short season rental of the barn (and not the house) at Treasure Farm. When a Los Angeles doctor informed Nan that she needed to have another major operation, the erstwhile comediennes decided to head for home in mid-August. Putting the best face on their disappointment, the girls wired a brief press notice to the *Kingston Daily Freeman* heralding their return: "Wilna Hervey and Nan Mason, who have been engaged on a motion picture by one of the Hollywood studios, left this morning to return to Woodstock."[7]

With Nan's notorious lead foot heavier on the gas pedal than usual, the erstwhile actresses made it across the continent in record time. The week's notice of their arrival was sufficient time, however, for one of their friends to devise the sort of welcome that could only occur in Woodstock and only for the Big Girls. Kaj Klitgaard, the Danish author and illustrator, who had moved to Bearsville with his wife, Georgina, two years before Wilna and Nan, took to his easel and created a tribute to their return.[8] Painted in gouache, Klitgaard's outrageous rendering shows Wilna and Nan as gigantic bare-breasted Amazons stepping over the nearby mountains into Woodstock to the joyful acclamation of the entire valley. "Woodstock ain't the same without you," reads one banner. Standing in the foreground, with their backs to the viewer, are three couples—the Speichers, the Klitgaards and the Rosens—all proclaiming, "We have missed you!" The fact that Elsie Speicher is shown waving a polka-dot hankie—one of Wilna's many recent gifts—must have pleased Wilna no end.

The reason for Nan Mason's second serious operation in eight years is unknown, though it appears to have been gynecological in nature. Facing considerable expense for the surgery, and having just spent more money than they ever made in Hollywood, Wilna and Nan had no choice but to liquidate some of their real estate to meet Nan's medical needs. Working long distance through an agent, Wilna disposed of one of their several Carmel properties in September. A few weeks later she sold a small parcel carved from one of her Bearsville properties. Nan's surgery in November was followed by a lengthy convalescence in a Manhattan hospital. Once she had sufficiently recovered and rested for several more weeks at home, the girls headed south for a long recuperative vacation in Florida on Anna Maria Island.[9]

The need to sell two properties to pay for a medical emergency makes it clear that by the late thirties Wilna Hervey and Nan Mason had essentially no savings or other liquid assets and thus no buffer against unexpected expenses. In the late twenties, flush with the windfall of their inheritances, they had assumed that Wilna's trust fund and Dan Mason's savings accounts would carry them easily through the years and that the income from their investments in real estate would be discretionary cash. But now, with Nan's nest egg and the Hervey Post Trust battered by the Depression, they had to rely on their real estate holdings to cover both monthly expenses and the cost of unforeseen emergencies. And while the several properties on two coasts brought in enough money to keep body and soul together, this modest income was badly managed. The cycle of feast and famine reflected in some of their surviving letters suggests either an inability or an outright unwillingness to budget their limited funds.

▲ ▲ ▲

In early September 1938 Wilna and Nan hosted a huge fundraising event at Treasure Farm to benefit the Woodstock Art Gallery. Illuminated only by the full moon and dozens of "family picnic" bonfires, the event was attended by hundreds of artists, writers, and musicians and their families decked out in costumes. As the evening wore on, and as the liquid refreshments flowed freely, impromptu orchestras and choruses filled the crisp autumn air.[10] If descriptions of the festive event sound more than a little like

FULL MOON
Costume Picnic
at Wilna's and Nan's
Friday Aug. 4th
6 P. M.

Please bring - Your Food
Your Drinks
Something to sit on
ALSO ANY PORTABLE MUSICAL
INSTRUMENT YOU PLAY
(No Oboes -- No Wind Instruments)

IF RAINY- COME SATURDAY
IF RAINY SATURDAY
THE HELL WITH IT!

Car Pooling Encouraged

Invitation to a Full Moon Costume Picnic. This postcard announcement for one of the girls' full moon parties likely dates from August 1944 when the full moon fell on a Friday. Intended as a substitute for the old Woodstock Maverick Festivals, the full moon parties at the home of Wilna and Nan became legends in their own right. The reason for their dislike of wind instruments in general, and oboes in particular, remains a mystery.

the legendary Maverick Festivals, it is because Wilna and Nan intended their "full moon" party to be a revival of that now defunct Woodstock tradition.

Hervey White's vaunted Maverick Festivals had been a victim of their own success. As the annual festival, held under the August full moon, grew in popularity (six thousand attendees in 1929), it gradually deteriorated, with bootleg booze fueling fights and instances of robbery and even rape convincing the local authorities that the event was getting out of hand. White was finally compelled to bring the tradition to an end in 1931. No one had mourned the demise of this annual community frolic more than Wilna and Nan, and it is not a surprise that they found a way to recreate it. Thus was born a new Woodstock tradition, the annual full moon party at the home of the Big Girls. Starting with this event in 1938, the yearly revel would continue, with only a few interruptions, for two decades.

It was typical of the increasingly bohemian lifestyle of the party girls of Bearsville that they had thrown this extravaganza in support of the local art gallery in spite of being unable to pay some of their own bills. Only two months after the September full moon beamed down upon Woodstock's finest cavorting through the meadows at Treasure Farm, Wilna and Nan were forced to take out a mortgage with the Ulster County Savings Institution, using their farm as collateral, to pay for the drilling of a new well. That they couldn't—or just didn't—pay more than seventeen dollars on that loan in the subsequent three years suggests the extent of their financial dysfunction.[11]

▲ ▲ ▲

Wilna's 1936 misadventures in Hollywood did not completely disabuse her of the notion that show business offered her a path to quick financial security. Shortly after she and Nan mortgaged Treasure Farm late in 1938, Wilna rented a small room in Manhattan so that she could seek out a way to exchange her acting talents for ready cash in some New York theater. If Hollywood didn't want her, perhaps Broadway did.

This new bid to keep the wolf from the door—or at least force him to knock several times—did not begin auspiciously. In their first month in Manhattan, Wilna's car died a dramatic and expensive death on Thirty-fourth Street, Nan was mugged in the subway and both of them came down with the flu. "New York will be the death of us, yet!" Wilna wrote to Leon Kroll, who was renting one of her studios in Bearsville while he worked on his WPA mural for the War Memorial Building in Worcester, Massachusetts. Pressed for cash to replace the bolts and gears that had fallen out of her car, and having no other source of funds, Wilna urged Kroll to send his next rent check immediately.[12]

The process of attending auditions and waiting—especially waiting—went on for months, with the frustration and tedium paralleling their previous ordeal in Los Angeles. Finally, in early July, Wilna tried out for and won the role of "The Biggest Girl" in a Broadway drama, *Summer Night*, scheduled to open at the St. James Theater in November 1939. Written by Vicki Baum, of *Grand Hotel* fame, and Benjamin Glazer, and staged by the legendary Lee Strasberg, *Summer Night* was based on the marathon dance craze of the late Depression years. The play was not a success. Denounced as a fiasco and a "floperoo," it folded after only four performances. One critic commented, "[E]xcellent actors and superb sets are wasted on this uninteresting and empty play."[13]

Disappointed to have endured four months of rehearsals only to appear on stage for four days, Wilna urged her agent to quickly find her another part. He did—a one-day gig as "Miss Santa Claus" at the Advertising Club's annual Christmas party at the Commodore Hotel. Though this "role" brought her more attention than her turn as The Biggest Girl, and got her picture in several newspapers, the realization that this was all she could get deflated Wilna's optimism sufficiently to finally convince her to abandon the theater. With considerable candor and understatement, she told a reporter who came to interview her as Miss Santa, "It's a little difficult getting parts."[14]

But Wilna wasn't done yet. If Broadway wasn't the answer, maybe broadcasting was. In that golden age of radio drama, Wilna considered the possibility that her rich contralto voice (albeit a bit husky from cigarette smoke) might land her a role in a radio play, a medium where her astonishing size wouldn't be a liability. But after weeks of more auditioning and waiting, she landed only a small, uncredited part in a minor drama broadcast from New York City the evening of February 24th, 1940. Listening from Woodstock, Caroline Rohland recognized Wilna only because of her laugh. "I hope something comes of it," she wrote her friend. But nothing did come of it and, after another month of fruitless searching, Wilna Hervey finally gave up her dream of making a fast buck in show biz and turned in the keys to her tiny apartment in Manhattan. Like gamblers who had stayed too long at the casino, she and Nan went back to their unresolved financial problems in Woodstock. Wilna had earned a total of seventy dollars, far less than she had spent on rent and sundry expenses while living in the city.[15]

CHAPTER 13

The War Years

Opposite: Wilna and Nan's Bearsville cottage. After the sale of Treasure Farm, the girls moved back to the "lower farm" and the modest house they had built in 1924. Apparently pleased with the improvements just made to her original Woodstock home in the mid-forties, Wilna cheerfully wrote on the back of this photo: "Isn't the house cute in the snow? You can see my plants in the kitchen window."[1]

Wilna's quixotic assault on the New York theatrical scene owed much to the fact that Nan got a job in Manhattan and worked every week of 1939. While we do not know what sort of employment she managed to find, Nan earned a total of four hundred and ninety dollars for her efforts. It wasn't a lot of money even by late Depression standards, but it helped pay the rent on their room and feed them while Wilna made the rounds of casting calls and audition halls. The paltry seventy dollars that Wilna earned as an actress in 1939 wasn't her total income. However, while she still had some cash flow from the rental of her remaining properties in Carmel and Woodstock, the payments from the Hervey Post Trust were increasingly disappointing. There are also indications that they may have lost one of the Carmel properties that March as a result of non-payment of taxes.[1]

Of course, the loss of another rental property meant that once again the girls lost a percentage of their total rental income. While the remaining holdings in Carmel had at least the potential to produce income (minus maintenance, taxes and fees for local rental agents), many of the Bearsville properties had become liabilities to the extent that, just as Dan Mason had warned Wilna years before, taxes were due on tracts that were not producing any income. While it had always been Wilna's intention to erect studios on all her lands and rent them to artists, this had not come to pass for a variety of reasons, among them the impracticality of some of the locations, the expense of doing so, a declining demand for rentals and Wilna's inconsistency in following through on her intentions. By 1940 the single biggest parcel—Treasure Farm—had become the single greatest burden, as the thirty-eight acres of the farm on the hill were now largely unused. Reluctantly, the erstwhile farmers began to wonder if the sale of Treasure Farm might be a prudent measure. But they prevaricated and procrastinated, unable to come to a decision, even after another unexpected expense forced them to take out an additional mortgage against the property in November 1941.[2] The following month, the decision to sell was made for them by an unlikely event: the Japanese bombing of Pearl Harbor.

Candis Hall Hitzig, Nan Mason, William Hitzig and Wilna Hervey at the Copacabana. As close friends of Bill and Candis Hitzig, the girls were frequently invited to spend weekends as their guests in Manhattan. When Bill Hitzig purchased Treasure Farm in 1942, he assured the girls that they would always be welcome there.

In 1934 Wilna had received a letter from an old friend, Candis Hall, who was honeymooning in Carmel-by-the-Sea. Hall, an intrepid aviatrix who in 1928 became the first woman to fly across the United States, as a passenger in an airmail plane, wrote to tell Wilna that she had married. "You're going to love my new husband," she predicted. Some months later, when the newlyweds made their first visit to Treasure Farm, the new husband, Dr. William M. Hitzig, looked down from the farmhouse at the panoramic view of meadows, orchards, and mountains and announced to his wife's friends that this was just the kind of place he would like to own. "Is it for sale?" he joked. Wilna was as charmed by Bill Hitzig as Candis had anticipated. And the feeling was mutual: Dr. Hitzig quickly developed a fondness for the two artists whose outlook and lifestyle were so refreshingly different from the high-pressure world of medical practice in Manhattan.[3] The two couples became close friends and frequently visited each other at Treasure Farm or at the fashionable Manhattan townhouse that Dr. Hitzig's ample income made possible.

With the entry of the United States into the Second World War in December 1941, the Hitzigs began to worry about the safety of their children living in a major population center that might be subject to attack. With the city installing air raid sirens and the Metropolitan Museum putting its more important pieces into storage, the doctor and his wife began to think about establishing a safe haven in the country. Aware of the difficulties their friends in Bearsville were having, and long enamored of Treasure Farm, they offered to buy the property.[4] By April 1942 the farm on the hill had new owners. The fact that they were transferring the property to friends with young children who would enjoy growing up there, and Bill Hitzig's promise—"I'll make it live, just as you would want it to live"—lessened the sting of giving up the homestead that Nan's father had helped them purchase. The Hitzigs made it clear that the girls were welcome at their old home at any time, a promise that was as sincere as it was gracious. In the years ahead, Wilna and Nan would go there in the summer to swim in the giant pool that the Hitzigs installed—the younger children loved riding on Wilna's back—and would often visit on Sunday night, Nan bringing along her ukulele so they could sing for their supper.[5]

The exiles of Treasure Farm returned to the lower farm and the little cottage they had built in 1924. The eight-acre property with a barn gave them ample room to garden and pasture any other animals they might wish to own, but was small enough to be manageable. Over the next three decades a large portion of the spacious grounds would be lovingly cultivated into a beautiful park with ornamental trees, flowering shrubs, massive beds of flowers and vegetable gardens.

Wilna and Nan on the grounds of their home. Adrian Siegel, a cellist with the Philadelphia Symphony Orchestra as well as an accomplished photographer famous for his photo-documentation of the orchestra in rehearsal, took this shot of Wilna and Nan enjoying the woodland setting they had carefully cultivated around their Bearsville cottage. Their house can be seen behind them.

Nan working as a house painter. When Wilna and Nan encountered financial problems during the Second World War, they turned to painting houses to raise much-needed cash. As artists with an eye for detail and precise manual skills, they were very successful in this new profession.

The financial straits that led the girls to sell Treasure Farm were desperate indeed. As a result of the ravages of the Depression, possibly compounded by poor management on the part of Wilna's increasingly erratic and irresponsible sister Eleanor, the Hervey Post Trust now provided Wilna with a mere pittance. "My bad sister had written and said I wasn't getting more than forty dollars a month," Wilna remembered. To raise some cash for essential needs, Wilna and Nan took up house-painting. With their contractor friend and neighbor Ishmael Rose finding them occasional jobs among his clients, they painted both interiors and exteriors. At least one senior citizen in Woodstock still remembers the remarkable sight of Wilna climbing up and down ladders carrying buckets of paint. It was an image worthy of a Toonerville skit. Predictably, it was Nan who dared to climb the highest ladders while Wilna cringed at the sight of her "Nannie" up on a roof.[6]

A more ambitious undertaking was the launching of the Gaylite Candles enterprise. Following up on a suggestion by the Woodstock ceramicist Carl Walters, who had once kept bill collectors at bay by selling candles he made, allegedly from pork-chop fat,

Wilna and Nan decided to begin crafting high-end tapers, forgoing pork tallow for the finest-quality ingredients. At first they tried making their colorful "polka dot and spiral" candles in the old chicken coop they had converted to a studio, but the high heat in such close quarters seemed risky. Subsequently they decided to rent a facility in Kingston with electric stoves that could be used to melt several big vats of paraffin at once. With temperatures in the room soaring to a hundred and ten degrees, Nan had to take salt pills to cope with her profuse sweating as she manufactured candles. Wilna had by now developed high blood pressure, a problem that would plague her for the rest of her life, and she soon found it impossible to work in the suffocating heat. She designed the label for the boxes, but candle making became a one-woman operation.[7]

Thanks to Nan's insistence on a forty percent content of stearic acid and her meticulous craftsmanship, her candles were accepted by Hammacher Schlemmer and several other prestigious stores in Manhattan. Nan also advertised that she would personally design candles to match discerning clients' table decorations.[8] The response was overwhelming. As the volume of orders mounted in advance of the Christmas season of 1942, Nan found herself besieged like the Sorcerer's Apprentice, frantically working all day and long into the night, barely keeping up with demand. Wilna did what she could, handling the boxing and shipping. When Nan emerged from her Kingston candle factory late on Christmas Eve, she was so exhausted that Wilna was alarmed by her pale and haggard appearance. A few months later, utterly done with candle

Box of Gaylite Candles. Pressed for funds in the early forties, the girls came up with the idea of making designer candles. This one surviving box of elegant tapers reflects Nan's high standards and craftsmanship. After more than seventy years, they still retain a faint but pleasant aroma of coconut, the result of the high stearic acid content she insisted upon. Wilna designed the box label, creating a childlike image that was somewhat at odds with the attempt to market the candles in upscale stores in Manhattan.

Three designs by Nan Mason. In the forties, Nan may have explored the possibility of taking on design commissions. These colorful oil studies of childlike repetitive patterns could have been templates for printing fabric or wallpaper. Sadly, nothing more is known about the original intentions for these pieces.

making, Nan sold the whole business to a tuberculosis sanitarium in upstate New York for three hundred dollars.[9]

Early in 1943 Nan moved on to another profession: construction supervisor and garden designer. In December of 1942 Juliana Force, long a frequent and welcome visitor to Woodstock, purchased the home of Carl Walters on Ohayo Mountain Road, just south of the center of Woodstock. Eager to transform the modest cottage into a home suitable for entertaining amidst her collections of art and antiques, Mrs. Force launched an ambitious scheme to enlarge the house and improve the grounds of the residence she christened "Laughing Waters."

Juliana Force had known Wilna Hervey and Nan Mason since the early thirties when they were introduced by their mutual friend Eugene Speicher. She quickly became very fond of them and invited them to parties in her fabled apartment with the lacquered chintz floor above the Whitney Museum. Her regard for the girls can be judged by the fact that when Wilna sat on one of her antique chairs and broke it, Juliana Force graciously told her, "I'd only be sad if it was our friendship that was broken."[10]

Aware of Nan's flair for design, and likely aware of the financial difficulties her friends were experiencing, she hired Nan to oversee the remodeling of her new Woodstock home, and to design a terrace and gardens. Trusting her judgment completely, Mrs. Force gave Nan her personal checkbook and complete authority to supervise renovations and pay the workmen if and when she was satisfied with their work. After Nan finished designing and laying out the new gardens, she was asked to stay on as groundskeeper.[11]

With the steady pay Nan was now receiving from Juliana Force, it became possible for the girls to make some much-needed improvements to their own house. Expanding both the bedroom and the kitchen of the cottage to provide more living space, they also installed large windows at both ends of the house, flooding the interior with abundant natural light for drawing and painting. The once cramped galley kitchen now terminated in a large eating area surrounded on three sides by windows offering a view of the gardens.[12]

During the war years, Wilna and Nan spent every winter in Bearsville, where their daily routines were heavily impacted by shortages. Like so many Americans who responded to President Roosevelt's "Food for Victory" campaign, the girls planted a "victory garden," expanding their usual summer plots of vegetables to even greater proportions. Ration stamps were needed to buy many essentials, such as coffee and sugar, but the girls were, remarkably enough, so circumspect in their purchases that they were able to share their coupons with Juliana Force when she ran out. They were fortunate to be heating their house with wood, and to have an adequate supply. The shortage of coal in Woodstock became so severe that some families were forced to move in together to keep warm. The cottage sheltering Wilna and Nan and their assortment of pets— four cats, two dogs, a bowl of goldfish, and a small flock of finches nesting and laying eggs in the house—was compact enough to require only a modest amount of fuel. This is not to say they were cozy. There are indications that the uninsulated dwelling could be chilly at times, a circumstance the girls accommodated by wearing layers of warm

Wilna Hervey gardening. That Wilna and Nan would plant a "victory garden" during the Second World War went without saying; it was just a matter of expanding their normally huge plot and growing more vegetables than ever.

clothing indoors and hanging blankets in the doorway to the bedroom to keep the heat from the fireplace insert from leaving the main living area. Gasoline rationing made it hard to get around even for routine chores, let alone casual socializing. Nan found it so difficult to obtain enough gas for the trips back and forth to her candle factory in Kingston that she had to petition the rationing board for an increase. A winter trip to Florida was out of the question.[13] Rather than waste precious fuel going in to Woodstock, the girls routinely hitched their mule to a small cart in dry weather, and to the sleigh when it snowed.

While Nan labored in her candle factory in temperatures that rivaled the tropics, Wilna endeavored to do her part for the war effort bundled up against an arctic blast. The possibility of another sneak air attack was a major concern in the aftermath of Pearl Harbor. When the U.S. Aircraft Warning Service set up an air observation outpost in Woodstock to give advance warning of any sneak attacks, volunteers were needed to watch and listen at all hours of the day and night. The spotters, headed up by the artist and herbalist Anita Smith, were given instructions in plane recognition and signed up to spend shifts of two to four hours in the small wooden building on stilts erected on Smith's property. During the notorious Catskill winters, a little wood-burning stove kept the volunteers from freezing to death as they peered out the open observation window. Wilna was

Winter sports. Bundled up against the frigid Woodstock weather, Wilna ventures out into the snow to entertain one of the cats by pulling it around on a sled. The barn that the girls built in 1925 can be seen in the background.

one of the many artists who spent time monitoring Woodstock's skies in defense of her country. Despite temperatures that dropped as low as thirty-two degrees below zero, and despite her considerable aversion to discomfort and her tendency to catch cold, Wilna signed up to take her turns watching for planes from the little tower.[14]

One casualty of the wartime gas rationing was Juliana Force. Unable to come and go as she wished, and increasingly ill with the onset of the cancer that would ultimately claim her, she decided to sell her Woodstock home in the fall of 1945. An advertisement for the property attracted the interest of a young Czech painter looking for a place to settle down with his family. As Nan continued to work at Laughing Waters as grounds-keeper, it was she whom William Pachner met when he went to see the place. They hit it off immediately. Not long after he purchased the house, Pachner and his wife, Lorraine, were invited to dine with Wilna and Nan.[15]

Impressed by his talent, and profoundly touched by his personal history—after the war he learned that he had lost his entire family, some eighty people, in the Holocaust— Wilna and Nan did everything they could to help the young couple assimilate into the world of Woodstock. They introduced the Pachners to the Speichers, the Rosens and other friends who were prominent in the arts community. But the Woodstock friendship that was to have the most far-reaching consequences for Pachner was his friendship with Wilna and Nan. In January 1951, when Pachner's financial situation became so desperate that he was close to giving up serious painting and returning to commercial art, Wilna took action. Spending the winter in Florida that season, she went to see her friend Georgine Shillard-Smith, an artist and philanthropist who had founded the Florida Gulf Coast Art Center in Clearwater. Shortly after Wilna's visit, Shillard-Smith invited Pachner to pay her a visit and subsequently hired him as an art instructor. It was a turning point in his career. Within two years the new art instructor was appointed curator of the Center and opened his own studio nearby. Sixty years later, Pachner's assessment of his friendship with Wilna and Nan was both simple and profound: "They changed my life."[16]

▲ ▲ ▲

On August 14th, 1945, came the welcome news that Japan had surrendered and at long last the Second World War was over. Within days, Wilna and Nan, ever quick to seize an opportunity to throw a party, were immersed in plans for a victory celebration. Not surprisingly, their soirée was a costume ball, and a fundraising vehicle for the girls' newest favorite charity, the Woodstock Health Center and its program to provide medical check-ups and free dental care for toddlers. Held at the Town Hall on August 31st, the ball featured dancing to the locally popular Fred Allen's Orchestra. In her announcement of the event, Wilna urged everyone "to be very gay" and offered prizes for the best costumes.[17]

Nan Mason, Pussy Cats. *Pen and ink drawing. The three cats piled on the comforter at the foot of Wilna and Nan's bed have a perfect view of the front yard and any passing traffic on Route 212. The modest cottage sheltered a number of pets at any given time. In those days, there was no such thing as a stray animal in Bearsville.*

William Pachner and Wilna Hervey. After the arrival of William Pachner in Woodstock in 1945, Wilna and Nan formed a close friendship with the painter, his wife, Lorraine, and their two children. Pachner described Wilna's intent gaze in this photograph as "a look of love."

The highlight of the evening, and the catalyst for raising money, was a feature that the girls had introduced at one of their full moon parties years before: a collaborative painting rendered by all of the artists present. A large blank canvas, thirty by sixty inches, was placed onstage and the artists in attendance paid for the opportunity to paint on it. When they finished, the completed spontaneous work was auctioned off.

The popularity of this feature can be judged by the fact that it was repeated at least a dozen times at subsequent parties hosted by Wilna and Nan in the forties and fifties. Over the years, the girls perfected the gimmick, learning that the level of participation, and therefore the sum raised, was in direct proportion to the volume of alcohol consumed. By waiting until the guests were thoroughly lubricated before setting up the canvas, they could depend on maximum enthusiasm on the part of Woodstock's veteran daubers when the time came for them to take up their brushes and show the crowd what they could do. The subsequent auctions to sell the freshly slathered composite works also tended to be more spirited and lucrative if the guests were feeling no pain. This inebriated approach to spontaneous painting did have its drawbacks, however. On at least one occasion, the last artist who paid to add his personal touches to the piece was so plastered that he painted over everything that the other artists had so carefully wrought.[18]

Remembering the Fallen

When gasoline rationing ended, and the Woodstock party circuit picked up steam again after the war, Wilna Hervey and Nan Mason seemed determined to make up for lost time. The girls shifted into full party mode, accepting any and all invitations, despite the fact that it aggravated Wilna's high blood pressure and two newly diagnosed stomach ulcers. Treatment for both of these conditions was largely ineffective in those days. Doctors addressed blood pressure issues by urging patients to diet, lose weight, stop drinking and stop smoking—dire measures that did not particularly appeal to Wilna. With her voracious appetite for good food, she did not last long on the "milk diet" that Dr. Hitzig prescribed for her stomach. Wilna's health, and her apparent disregard for it, were enough of a concern by 1946 that one of her closest friends, Fritzi Striebel, begged her to take a break. The wife of the celebrated "Dixie Dugan" comic strip creator, John Striebel, Fritzi wrote to Wilna after reading her description of a wild escapade combined with complaints of her ulcer acting up: "You *must* take care of yourself," she warned Wilna. "Can't you just be quiet for a while + say no to all parties? *Please do!*" Her plea fell on deaf ears. Wilna would rather attend a party, and be forced to lie down on her host's bed for a while to catch her breath, than risk missing out on the fun.[1]

Typical of their inability to refuse any invitation, or miss any chance to gather with friends, was the twelve-hour gastronomic marathon Wilna and Nan indulged in on Thanksgiving Day 1947. Starting with a midday dinner with the Hitzig family at Treasure Farm, the girls moved on in the early evening to a second turkey dinner with Charles Rosen's family and their guests, then finished the day by attending a large party thrown by the Striebels.

John and Fritzi Striebel were entertaining some of the girls' favorite people that evening. In attendance were the younger generation of cartoonists and illustrators, including David Huffine, Carl Hubbell, and John Pike and their wives, all of whom had come to

Woodstock during the war. Admirers of his longstanding syndicated comic strip, the younger Woodstock "inkers" tended to cluster around Striebel and regard him as their leader. The Striebels' Thanksgiving party concluded with two more large turkeys served at midnight. "O! God! I felt so stuffed I didn't eat for 2 days," Wilna wrote to Philadelphia Orchestra cellist Adrian Siegel and his wife, Sophie. "But we did have a good time!" Asked about their perpetual motion social lives in a late-life interview, Nan offered a simple explanation: "We just love people."[2]

But the war also brought out a serious side of Wilna that no one had seen before. During the conflict, more than two hundred Woodstock area residents saw military service, many of them the sons of local artists, musicians and writers whom she knew. A dozen young men from the community did not return. Wilna was deeply saddened by the loss of these servicemen and empathized with the grief of the families. Channeling her feelings into action, she decided that Woodstock needed to honor its war dead in some tangible and meaningful way. Thus in 1947 Wilna became, for the first and only time in her life, a community activist.

Beginning with conversations at the August 1947 revival of the Maverick Festival (a tightly controlled experiment to see if it might be "safe" to stage the legendary parties again), Wilna began to contact every major civic, religious, and professional figure in the community and invite them to join her in forming a committee to explore the creation of a war memorial on the village green. In the process, she demonstrated energy and leadership skills that many might not have expected her to possess. Woodstock's town supervisor signed on early, and twenty-one local organizations—among them the Woodstock Guild of Craftsmen, the American Legion, the Lutheran and Methodist churches, the Red Cross and the Woodstock Market Fair—were represented at the first meeting Wilna arranged, on September 26th, 1947. After agreeing to form a permanent organization to be known as the Woodstock War Memorial, the group unanimously elected Wilna president of the new enterprise.[3]

The Woodstock War Memorial organization formed committees to handle the various important issues to be confronted—raising money, soliciting designs, building an athletic field with any

Marianne Greer Appel, Plan for the Woodstock War Memorial. *Of all the plans submitted, the understated and dignified design by the young Marianne Greer Appel was selected by the War Memorial Committee. The memorial can still be seen on Woodstock's village green.*

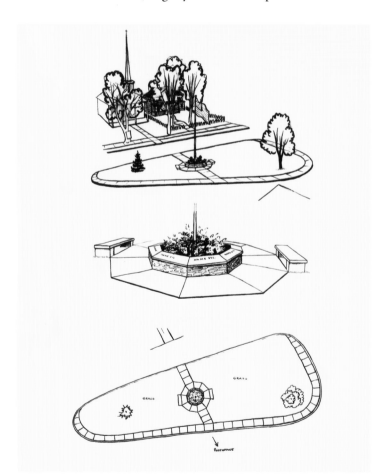

leftover funds, and recruiting the skilled help needed for the actual construction of the monument and athletic field. Wilna sat with each of these committees at their several meetings, making a valiant effort to actually keep track of details. She also found herself obliged to smooth over a number of difficulties as they arose. The planned memorial was not universally welcomed nor without opposition. Since the monument was proposed to sit in front of the venerable Dutch Reformed Church—which Wilna and Nan occasionally attended—members of that congregation expressed concern that "whatever is put on the village green should in every way harmonize with the church." At one uncomfortable public meeting, Wilna was confronted by a disgruntled member of the American Legion who claimed that the Legion membership was against the memorial (in fact, they were not) and insisted that a public monument would bring only sadness to the families of the lost men.[4] Wilna enjoyed the support of some very influential local allies, like the pastor of the Dutch Reformed Church and the commander of the American Legion, both of whom strongly backed her up on such occasions.

When the community at large was invited to submit designs, ideas and plans poured in. By early November, it was the "dignified and unassuming" design put forward by Marianne Greer Appel that was unanimously chosen by the organization. Appel's concept called for a large, ten-sided bluestone base, filled with earth, supporting a flagpole and surrounded by benches. Wrapped around the base of the flagpole, two bronze plaques would bear the names of all twenty-eight of Woodstock's war dead since the Civil War.[5]

Fundraising now began in earnest, and continued throughout the winter. Along with all her other duties, Wilna participated in the solicitations, going door-to-door, even in terrible weather. Inevitably, the strain of this nonstop effort, an exertion that provided none of the endorphin release that accompanied strenuous partying, began to take its toll, and Wilna, who had a long history of stress-related illnesses, began to falter. "Wilna Hervey has been ill this past week but hopes that she will be well enough to call a meeting of the war memorial association," ran one ominous item in the local paper in January 1948. Two months later, with her ulcers unbearable and her blood pressure raging out of control, Wilna sadly and reluctantly tendered her resignation as president of the organization she had founded. Reflecting the extraordinary effort she had made up to that point, and the extent to which it was appreciated, the memorial group immediately and unanimously voted to make Wilna honorary president.[6]

Wilna and "Buster Brown." As a gesture of support for Wilna's work with the War Memorial Committee, William Hitzig gave the girls this pony as a gift. Buster Brown brought years of joy to Wilna and Nan's lives. The look on Wilna's face speaks volumes about her love of animals in general and for this tiny creature in particular.

Wilna Hervey, Santa and the Pony. *Watercolor. Wilna celebrated the arrival of Buster Brown with this small painting of Santa Claus delivering the pet. It helps to know that Dr. Hitzig, who paid for the pony, sometimes dressed up as Santa Claus on Christmas morning and dropped in on his neighbors, including Wilna and Nan.*

Stepping out of the active presidency did not end Wilna's involvement with the memorial organization, however. Later that summer she staged a baseball game to score more of the money needed for both the monument and the athletic field.[7] The August 21st contest pitted a team of Woodstock artists against a team of Woodstock writers and musicians, several of whom had been begged, cajoled and pressured by Wilna into participating. "Wilna could be very persuasive," Bill Pachner remembered, "and not just because of her size." Taking advantage of the fact that the popular British actor Arthur Treacher was appearing in *The Magistrate* at the local playhouse, Wilna drafted him to take part as well. Treacher showed up wearing judicial robes and, though more familiar with cricket than American baseball, proceeded to make rulings as the umpire, considerably complicating the job of the real umpire, the writer Henry Morton Robinson. The five hundred spectators who gathered to watch the artists lose fifteen to nothing contributed nearly four hundred dollars to the cause. Earlier that same week, Wilna and Nan hosted their annual costume party and picnic at their home and collected from their guests another sixty dollars for the memorial fund.[8]

Wilna's role in the creation of the War Memorial raised her already high profile in the Woodstock community, and for several years, starting in late 1947, the *Kingston Daily Freeman* reported nearly every social event that she and Nan attended. No activity was considered so minor that the general readership didn't deserve some notification. When the girls attended an animal-film party at the home of Mrs. Milne, went to New York City to attend the opening of an art exhibition, or had dinner at the home of Maud and Miska Petersham, the outing was written up for public consumption. Even the news that Wilna shot a porcupine that invaded her garden was reported in detail, as was the arrival days later of Eugene and Elsie Speicher, who had been invited to dinner. Fortunately for the Speichers, these last two reports were unrelated.[9]

During one of her publicized visits to Manhattan to spend the weekend with the Hitzigs, Wilna received a surprise that may have been, at least in part, a gesture of support and approval for her efforts on behalf of the War Memorial. Over the weekend as they dined and attended Broadway plays with their friends, Dr. Hitzig heard the girls talking about ponies. At breakfast the next morning, he reached into his pocket, pulled out a roll of bills and began peeling them off. Putting a pile of money in front of both Wilna and Nan, he told them, "Go buy yourselves a pony." Days later, at a horse sale in Kingston, they found the perfect pet. "There before our eyes, as if made to order for us, was the pony," Wilna wrote to Adrian and Sophie Siegel of her discovery. "So gentle and cute—with beautiful mane & tail & bangs & beautiful soft brown eyes." Buster Brown, as Wilna named him, was so tiny that his proud owners walked him on a leash like a dog. For the youngest residents of Woodstock he would be a local celebrity for years to come. Wilna hitched the pony to a little cart and went up and down the streets and lanes of Woodstock giving rides to all the children she could find. When Nan took Buster Brown to the Woodstock Library Fair, boys and girls lined up for a chance to climb upon his miniature saddle and take a short canter around the grounds.[10]

Early in 1949 enough money had finally been raised to have the two plaques with the names of Woodstock's war dead designed and cast in bronze. With the plaques in place at the base of the flagpole by summer, the memorial was officially dedicated on the Fourth of July. Dr. James Shotwell, president of the Carnegie Endowment for International Peace and a Woodstock resident, delivered the keynote address. In reporting the event, the local newspaper paid tribute to Wilna Hervey, who, in the fall of 1947, had begun the process that created the memorial. Wilna would later say that she considered the creation of the Woodstock War Memorial the proudest achievement of her life.[11]

Konrad Cramer, The Woodstock War Memorial on the Village Green. *Not long after the dedication ceremony, Cramer captured the simple dignity of the memorial with its plaques commemorating Woodstock's war dead since the Civil War.*

CHAPTER 15

"Something New, Something Different"

Opposite: Wilna Hervey, Landscape. *Watercolor. Though the scene bears some similarity to the property where the girls lived after selling Treasure Farm, the landscape is a generic view of Bearsville. Wilna presented this painting to Nan on her fiftieth birthday in July 1946.*

N an Mason's various jobs left her little time to paint or draw in the years just before and during the war, and she contributed no new works to any of the wartime exhibitions in Woodstock. Wilna Hervey, on the other hand, enjoyed a period of relative inspiration and creativity in the same time frame. Two portraits that Wilna did in the early forties survive today, one a charcoal sketch of a Hispanic man and the other an oil portrait of an African-American woman. Twenty years after her first encounter with Winold Reiss, Wilna was still his devoted follower, studying ethnic "types." But these works would prove to be the last gasp of Reiss's influence on Wilna. Mindful of Henry Lee McFee's exhortation a few years earlier to find her own style, Wilna had begun to toy with a new approach, one that sprang from the core of her unique personality and simultaneously embraced and flouted the rules of art she had labored so long to learn and perfect. This new mode of representation, with which Wilna would be identified for the rest of her life, appeared for the first time just after the war in a series of paintings and drawings of local subjects such as the Woodstock post office, the village green and a rodeo sponsored by the Woodstock Riding Club. Usually modest in size and rendered in mixed media or watercolors, Wilna's new works were done in a style that was described by one associate as "exuberant primitivism."[1] Like the artist herself, her new style was warm, childlike and accessible, and harbored an occasional inexplicable quirk.

In addition to Wilna's new stylistic explorations, the late forties saw both of the girls making their first experiments with fine art photography. They had been avid photographers for decades, even in the days when all they had available was a basic Kodak Brownie. Several invoices from the thirties for supplies bought at The Little Art Shop—a Woodstock emporium for all things artistic as well as pharmaceuticals, candy, dry goods and sundries—show ongoing charges for film, developing and printing that rival the amounts they were spending on their staple purchases of ice cream, cigarettes,

Right: Wilna Hervey, Portrait of an Unidentified Black Woman. *Oil on canvas. A great shift in style can be seen from Wilna's realistic portrait of an unidentified African-American woman to her rendering of the Woodstock post office and the village green just a few years later.*

Wilna Hervey, The Woodstock Post Office. *Mixed media. As Wilna's new naïve style emerged in the years after the war, her subject matter was exclusively drawn from her familiar surroundings. This view of downtown Woodstock is notably more cautious than her rendering of the village green done a year later.*

candy and popcorn. But it wasn't until the postwar period that either Wilna or Nan began to move beyond taking snapshots and seriously explore the medium of photography as fine art. When they did, the results were striking. As was so often the case with her new pursuits, Nan quickly learned developing and printing techniques and rapidly achieved an impressive level of skill. She is even reported to have won at least one award for her photography in the late forties, though, unfortunately, no further details are known.[2]

Wilna Hervey, The Village Green. *Gouache. Throwing caution (and at least one traditional rule of art) to the wind, Wilna explored a dramatically different approach as she experimented with her new style. Only the careful articulation of the human figures reveals a trained artist behind this exuberant and whimsical rendering.*

Wilna Hervey, Rodeo. *Oil painting. Just after the Second World War, a series of Western-style rodeos were held at the Lake Hill Arena, not far from Bearsville. Wilna and Nan, who had been ardent supporters of the sponsoring organization, the Woodstock Riding Club, attended the events. The cowboy shown is possibly the performer Bud Nelson on his trick horse Butterscotch; both were celebrities at the rodeos.*

Nan's photographic explorations in the late forties and early fifties paralleled those of several of her Woodstock friends; Caroline Rohland, Adrian Siegel, Konrad Cramer and Manuel Komroff all had begun to investigate this medium as a possible new outlet for their creative energies. When Nan won an award of four hundred and fifty dollars for creativity from the Woodstock Foundation in October 1951, the cash (more than three thousand dollars in today's money) went a long way toward remodeling the old chicken coop and erstwhile candle factory as a darkroom and studio. By 1952 Nan was exhibiting her photos alongside those of her friends and her works were being well received. Though she preferred to paint, Wilna also produced enough of her own photographs that, in the spring of 1953, both of the girls could join Konrad and Florence Cramer in entering works in the Hudson Valley Photographers Show at New Paltz State Teachers College.[3]

Early in 1953, when Nan attended classes in silk screening offered by Jerry Jerominek at the Woodstock Guild of Craftsmen,[4] she applied this new skill to an avocation that occupied much of her own and Wilna's time and energy each fall: the creation of Christmas cards. Exchanging personally designed and crafted cards was an important and longstanding holiday tradition for the Woodstock artists; a rich collection of these seasonal art works has been preserved by the Historical Society of Woodstock. While Wilna would still spend all day hand-painting special cards for one or two of their closest friends, henceforth the bulk of the Christmas mail they took to the Bearsville post office each December would consist of silk-screened imagery that Wilna devised and Nan printed. Without exception, Wilna's designs for their personal greeting cards featured drawings of the two artists, and sometimes their pets as well, in seasonal tableaux.

Nan Mason, Rondout Ferry Slip. *As Nan began to explore the possibilities of art photography, she returned to the harbor at Rondout, near Kingston, which had inspired her print of the tugboats in 1932.*

Wilna and Nan at a country fair. As the girls make their way through the exhibits at a local fair, Nan wears two cameras around her neck, cases open and ready for action.

Wilna Hervey, Nan. Along with the piano, ukulele, guitar and banjo, Nan learned to play the accordion. This is the only formal portrait of Nan intended for public consumption that Wilna ever created. Nan was fifty-five years old at the time.

On her annual Christmas cards,
Wilna usually portrayed herself, Nan
and the pets in seasonal tableaux.
While scenes of sledding, bringing
home the Christmas tree, or sitting
around in their bathrobes on
Christmas morning were based on real
life events, Wilna could not resist an
occasional flight of fancy, such as the
image of her and Nan riding through
the heavens on huge geese. The Florida
Express card shows their final pet, a
very spoiled Siamese cat named Choi,
tucked in her carrier and ready to
head south for the holidays.

Wilna discovered the genre for which she is best remembered today in the mid-fifties, and somewhat by accident. Intent on brightening up the interior of her home with colorful switch plates, she enrolled in a popular adult education course in enameling offered by the Woodstock Guild of Craftsmen and taught by Joan Pond. In learning this new craft, Wilna progressed through the usual beginner's assortment of earrings and ashtrays before advancing to the stage of expertise needed to create the switch plates she had envisioned. By the time she had achieved her initial goal, she had become so intrigued by the process of enameling that she began to experiment with the idea of creating tiny enamel "paintings" of animals, children and flowers.

The process of enameling is fraught with peril for the novice, and there is much to be learned through experience and experimentation. With enameling, instead of brushing pigments onto the surface, one must carefully push a paste of powdered glass mixed with a little water into position, a process that requires a different but equally demanding form of manual control and precision as painting. However, one cannot produce new shades of color simply by mixing enamels, as one would with pigments when working in oils or watercolors. The same enamel might provide different results, depending on where and how it is applied—directly onto the bare copper, over a previously fired layer of translucent or opaque white enamel, or over slips of gold or silver foil—and how the piece is fired. The author of the standard text on enameling used in Wilna's time recommended making a series of small test plaques to be kept on hand for quick reference, and admitted that the artist usually doesn't know what value of color is going to emerge until the work comes out of the kiln. Sometimes, several layers of enamel have to be applied to the same area and repeatedly fired before the desired color tone is achieved. As there is no way to know for certain how long each firing will take to achieve the desired result, one must frequently peek into the kiln to see what is transpiring. Understandably, many of Wilna's first efforts were not so aesthetically pleasing. But, excited by the possibilities and determined to perfect this genre to which her naïve style of painting translated so beautifully, Wilna pressed on.[5]

Wilna Hervey, Switch Plate with Enamel Décor. *It was the crafting of enameled switch plates that started Wilna on the artistic endeavor that would bring her recognition in her later years. This particular piece was found still mounted on the wall in the ruins of the girls' chicken coop-turned-studio in Bearsville.*

A section of the chicken coop/candle factory/darkroom now became a small enameling studio. Wary of fire after their experience with candle making in the confined space, Wilna covered the workbench, floors and walls with a thick layer of

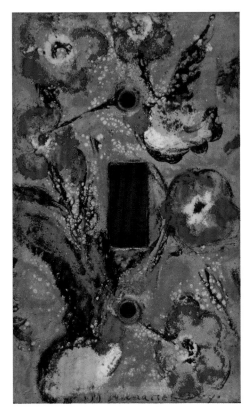 

Wilna's transition from purely decorative switch plates to miniature enamel paintings can be seen in these two pieces that foreshadow the multitude of paintings of floral arrangements and narrative scenes she would produce throughout the sixties and seventies.

Above left: Wilna Hervey, Enameled Switch Plate with Scene of Flowers and Hummingbirds. *Not wanting the screw holes in the plates to interfere with her composition of birds and flowers, Wilna resourcefully positioned the two hummingbirds so that the holes would become their eyes. It is likely that she completed the effect by painting the screw heads once the plate was installed.*

Above right: Wilna Hervey, Enameled Switch Plate with Scene of Mother and Children. *Family scenes would become a frequent motif of Wilna's enamel paintings. Here she shows a mother with two little boys, the balls they're playing with carefully located over the two screw holes in the plate. The fact that she signed both of these plates is an indication that she was already thinking of her switch plates as miniature paintings and not purely utilitarian or decorative objects.*

asbestos to protect against the heat of her little kiln and the scorching hot metals that would be withdrawn from it. The tools that lined her workbench reflected the improvisational nature of Wilna's new venture. There was a flat steel automobile spring she used to transport works in and out of the kiln, a dental tool she commandeered from her dentist for moving the wet enamel paste, and—evoking memories of Powerful Katrinka—a seventy-five-pound section of railroad track that she used as a weight to keep newly fired

Wilna Hervey, The Library Fair. *One of the most charming of Wilna's "learning steps," this enamel painting shows the "Great Expectations Booth" at the annual library fair in Woodstock. Wilna discovered that her naïve style was well suited to the medium of enamel painting.*

Wilna Hervey, Hunt's Circus. *Enamel. With their enthusiasm for animals and clowns, both Wilna and Nan looked forward to the arrival of the circus as much as any of Woodstock's children. Hunt's Circus was based in nearby Kingston and performed locally every year. Wilna's composition allows the bulk of the elephants to echo the mass of the Big Top and the mountains in the distance.*

Left: Wilna Hervey, Little Girl with Cats. *Enamel. One of the noteworthy quirks of Wilna's primitive style was that, in spite of her considerable skill as a portrait artist, she rarely provided facial features on human figures in her watercolors and enamels.*

Below: Nan Mason, Godchild. *Their love of children is reflected in many of Nan's photographs as well as in Wilna's paintings and enamels. Nan captured this image of Wilna walking on the beach at Anna Maria Island, Florida, with their three-year-old godchild. This little boy had been baptized in a ceremony held under the trees on their Bearsville property.*

Left: Wilna Hervey, Child with Lollipop. *Watercolor. Wilna and Nan doted on their friends' children and grandchildren, occasionally even dressing up as clowns to entertain them. This tiny portrait reflects not only Wilna's affection for the unidentified little boy but also her lifelong fondness for miniature paintings.*

Above: Nan Mason, Manhattan Skyline. *Enamel on copper, triptych. On occasion both Wilna and Nan created diptych and triptych panoramas by joining together enamel panels. This is one of the finest of Nan's enamel works.*

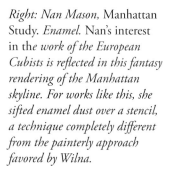

Right: Nan Mason, Manhattan Study. *Enamel. Nan's interest in th*e *work of the European Cubists is reflected in this fantasy rendering of the Manhattan skyline. For works like this, she sifted enamel dust over a stencil, a technique completely different from the painterly approach favored by Wilna.*

pieces from warping. On the asbestos walls she framed and hung her "learning steps" so that she could see where she had come from and where she was going. She considered this visual record of her progress sacrosanct. When visitors in later years asked if the best of her learning steps might be for sale, she reacted with horror: "I couldn't sell these paintings . . . They are precious."[6]

Many in Wilna's circle were impressed by her new creations, none more so than Eugene Speicher, who watched with growing delight as each new batch of his friend's

Right: Nan Mason, Rainy Day. *Colored pencil drawing. Nan's inventiveness and flair for design can be seen here as she goes from the literal to the abstract in her treatment of a rainy day in Manhattan.*

Left: Nan Mason, Umbrellas. *Gouache. In both of these pieces, the identities of frantic pedestrians are hidden beneath their umbrellas as they dash along city streets in the rain. The whimsical touch of adding a dog, oblivious to the storm as he contemplates a fire hydrant, is typical of Nan's sense of humor.*

enamel paintings achieved higher levels of finesse and artistic appeal. "Keep at it," he urged Wilna. "You've discovered something new, something different!"[7]

Nan, of course, soon tried her hand at enamel painting. Given her flair for design and her interest in cubist-inspired compositions, many of Nan's crisp and linear enamel paintings were vastly different from Wilna's dreamy evocations. She also appears in several instances to have used a technique different from that preferred by Wilna: sifting dry powdered glass over stencils carefully placed on a copper plate that had been sprayed with

Nan Mason, The Fifth Avenue Bus. *Pencil sketch. Nan grew up in and around New York City. Her fascination with Manhattan and with city life was longstanding and the inspiration for numerous works, both literal and abstract.*

a weak solution of gum tragacanth. Long fascinated by the New York City skyline, Nan did a series of cityscapes, some literal and others quite stylized. Eventually Nan also began to experiment with crafting enameled bowls, a genre for which she would win recognition. These were often presented as gifts and several of her old friends still display theirs.

▲ ▲ ▲

By the nineteen-fifties Wilna had several chronic health conditions that would plague her the rest of her days. In addition to her high blood pressure and ulcers, she had begun to suffer hip problems due to arthritis, was trending toward diabetes, and had kidney ailments and gallbladder flare-ups. She also had dental problems and on one occasion an infected tooth triggered symptoms that were at first mistaken for signs of more serious health issues. Her refusal to let these conditions slow her down amazed some of her friends. "I don't believe our Willie is ever comfortable," Elsie Speicher wrote to Fritzi Striebel, "and yet she remains so sweet and loving . . . always."[8]

In January 1954 Wilna had a bout of illness serious enough to land her in a New York City hospital, where the staff's inability to find a bed big enough for her added to her misery.[9] This intimation of mortality may have been the catalyst that spurred Wilna to finally act on an idea she had toyed with since the late forties. She decided to write her memoirs, concentrating heavily on her one-time celebrity as Powerful Katrinka and Tillie Olson. Even after her frustrations in Hollywood in 1936 and her failure to conquer Broadway in 1939, Wilna still had not abandoned the notion that her acting career held the potential to reward her with financial success. Now she hoped that a humorous recounting of her silent-movie days would become a bestseller and allow her and Nan to finally get their heads above the financial waters for good.

While Wilna was a very good writer herself, she felt that her memoir would benefit from the services of a professional who was skilled at both writing and marketing. She sought the assistance of Karin Lindin Whiteley, the adopted daughter of her old friends Carl Eric and Louise Lindin. Wilna had known Karin since she was a baby. Now in her early forties and a divorced mother with one son, Karin Whiteley had once worked as a literary agent and was currently employed at the public relations firm of Dudley, Anderson, Yutzy in Manhattan. She agreed to help her old friend with the project.[10]

Wilna began writing up her memories by hand on long sheets of yellow paper, noting down everything she could remember, consulting Nan, who had witnessed much of the movie-making, and writing to old friends. Karin Whiteley typed up Wilna's drafts, improved them, and asked more questions. She also tried to sort out Wilna's tendency to confuse both the titles of her old movies and the roles she had played in them. Accompanied by her co-author, Wilna went to visit Fontaine Fox in September 1957 and spent the day reminiscing about the Toonerville films and gathering details for her book. She was pleased that he approved of her intended title, "The Original Katrinka."[11]

By the spring of 1959 a forty-five-page manuscript had been produced, covering the Toonerville and Plum Center years, with an outline of what was to follow. Wilna's collaborator felt they had enough, with the typescript and a portfolio of old production stills, to begin shopping it around to agents: "If there is interest, we would probably get an advance and a contract." But, she warned Wilna, "don't start counting chickens. We're still a long way from anywhere."[12] Her warning was prescient.

In the next two years the book proposal went to one publisher after another. Rejection letters arrived in turn from St. Martin's Press, Hall, Doubleday, Norton, Viking Press and Triangle Publishing. While Karin Whiteley calmly accepted each refusal as just part of the process and immediately sent the manuscript on to the next target, Wilna became increasingly frustrated and agitated with their lack of success and began to take personal offense at each new disappointment. "You make me almost afraid to send you the comments I get because you take it all so seriously," her co-author told Wilna at one point after receiving a particularly baroque lamentation from the artist formerly known as Katrinka. "Sometimes books travel to 18 different publishers before someone nibbles," she reassured her. But, in fact, there would be no nibbles at all. When Karin Whiteley lost her job at Dudley, Anderson, Yutzy in March 1961 she became too preoccupied with her own problems to spend more time on Wilna's book. Later that year Wilna wrote to Norman Cousins, editor-in-chief of the *Saturday Review*, whom she had met through their mutual friend, Dr. Hitzig. Pointing out that Whiteley felt a professional ghostwriter might be necessary for her memoirs, Wilna asked Cousins if he would take a look at her manuscript. What sort of reply she got is unknown, but it appears that the project came to an end shortly thereafter. While Wilna and Karin continued to correspond for the rest of Wilna's life, the book that they once thought would "fill a certain gap" in early film history never came to pass. Wilna Hervey would go on telling the tales of her glory days in the movies for the rest of her life, but those stories would not appear in print during her lifetime.[13]

CHAPTER 16

"We Have Learned to Be Practical"

Opposite: Wilna Hervey, Breakfast with the Pets. *Watercolor. Wilna's art was often inspired by the domestic world she shared with Nan. In this piece, based on a photograph she took in their kitchen, Wilna changed the shape and proportions of the chair she is seated in to suggest that it is sagging under her weight.*

Because of the demands of the memoir project, Wilna Hervey and Nan Mason had remained in Bearsville year-round in the late fifties, enduring several harsh winters in a row. The winter of 1958/59 was especially unpleasant, even by Woodstock standards, with relentless snow and one all-out blizzard. Wilna, now in her mid-sixties and plagued by arthritis and high blood pressure, found the snow-shoveling and other winter tasks more than she could handle.[1]

Although confined to their small cottage for months by snow and ice, the two artists were never in danger of contracting cabin fever. Even when they weren't painting, tweaking photographs, crafting silver jewelry or creating enamels, both of them were compulsive sketchers, constantly drawing or at least doodling on any available surface. Backs of envelopes, the flip side of a placemat from Howard Johnson's, cardboard panels cut from the inside of cereal boxes, and the reverse side of bills they neglected to pay all served as grounds for impromptu renderings of ideas or images that had piqued their interest. The large number of works—both casual and formal—that date from this period indicates just how many days and weeks they were forced to spend indoors during those four winter seasons.

The frozen conditions inspired a number of Wilna's pieces, but for the most part she chose to portray her daily life indoors, using herself, Nan and their pets as her models. In the process, she documented the interior of their Bearsville home and the relaxed lifestyle they enjoyed there. Perhaps consciously, Wilna was documenting a domestic scene that was about to undergo a substantial change.

When Wilna first came to Woodstock in the summer of 1918 she was compelled to live in a barn, as nothing else was available. Four decades later she ended up living in a barn once again, though this time it was the result of a conscious decision. By the late fifties the little barn that Wilna and Nan had built in the twenties was empty for the first time ever. When the last of their large animals, their beloved Buster Brown, went to his

Above: Wilna Hervey, The Bearsville Cottage in Winter. *Watercolor. As a delivery boy approaches the Bearsville cottage with a bag of groceries for the girls, one of the dogs has come out to greet him. The piece is typical of the dozens of little sketches Wilna routinely did as a kind of visual diary without any intention of ever showing them to anyone.*

Right: Wilna Hervey, The Blizzard of '58. *Watercolor. Wilna and Nan have just parked their car in the garage beside the barn and are walking to the house, circled by their excited dogs. On one occasion during that awful winter, they managed to get out for groceries only because some local men they knew agreed to come by and spread sand over the ice-covered road to provide them some traction.*

reward, the girls decided to forgo the demanding chores and expense of keeping large pets. With no further need for a barn as such, they had the ground level of the building remodeled as a small apartment that could be rented to artists as a studio. They financed this construction by selling a parcel of land in Bearsville to their friends Theodore Wassmer and his wife, Judy Farnsworth Lund, two artists who had come to Woodstock several years earlier.[2]

For a couple of years the little barn studio was rented seasonally. Then Wilna and Nan concluded that it made more sense for them to move into the barn themselves. They rented the cottage to John B. Houlder, a tall, strapping Norwegian designer and crafts-man who agreed to work on the property as groundskeeper in partial payment of the rent. He and his wife, Dr. Marie Lien Houlder, would live in the cottage for years and help maintain the park the girls had created all around their home. Their presence also provided Wilna and Nan with a sense of security when they were in residence and peace of mind when they were out of town.[3]

Wilna's chronic ailments likely informed their conclusion that it was time to sim-plify their lives. Even though the living space in their cottage had never been especially large, downsizing into the barn apartment meant an even tighter squeeze that required them to discard some of their furniture. Their spinet piano was one of the casualties, though Nan's accordion, guitar and ukulele remained to provide them with music. One thing not discarded was Wilna's voluminous collection of letters, photographs, movie memorabilia and personal artifacts. Her archive already filled a small garage on the prop-erty. The rest of it now went into the spacious loft above the apartment, where it contin-ued to grow and where—according to a young man recruited years later to retrieve an

Wilna Hervey, Ice Skating. *Enamel on copper diptych. For obvious reasons, Wilna was leery of venturing out onto the ice herself, regardless of how thick it seemed. She loved to watch the children skating, however. Here, she captures their energy and enjoyment with a series of caricatures reminiscent of Fontaine Fox's drawings of his* Toonerville Folks.

Right and opposite: Wilna Hervey, Two Women at the Piano, *two versions. As can be seen in these two portraits of herself and Nan at the piano, Wilna sketched out her compositional ideas in watercolor before tackling a subject in enamel. Their little piano was one of the casualties of their move to the small apartment in the barn.*

antique cast-iron sewing machine from the hoard—her accumulated treasures took on the look and mystique of King Tut's tomb.[4] The little barn studio would be their primary residence for the rest of their lives.

The annual costume picnics that Wilna and Nan had staged for more than twenty years were also destined for some downsizing, but not before one last hurrah that outdid all the rest. To celebrate the Fourth of July 1959, Woodstock's favorite party hostesses invited so many guests to attend their festivities that the county sheriff felt it prudent to send an officer to the normally placid hamlet of Bearsville to control traffic. Under colorful lights strung throughout the trees in their park by two of the older Hitzig boys, Wilna and Nan staged a costume

parade, complete with music and an announcer, and awarded prizes to recipients determined by a panel of judges. As usual, various local musicians played and sang throughout the evening; there was jazz and there were folksongs. But the main musical entertainment for this festival was provided by the Turnau Opera Players, a company of professional performers that had taken up residence in Byrdcliffe a couple of years before. The Turnau group offered a half-hour-long program that included scenes from *Die Fledermaus* as well as arias from *Carmen* and *Kiss Me, Kate*. The girls' longstanding tradition of using the party to drum up support for one of their favorite causes was not forgotten. As enthusiastic fans of the Turnau Opera Players, they made sure everyone knew about the opera programs that were scheduled for the rest

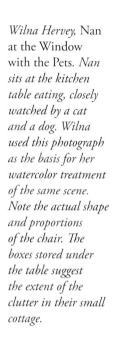

Wilna Hervey, Nan at the Window with the Pets. *Nan sits at the kitchen table eating, closely watched by a cat and a dog. Wilna used this photograph as the basis for her watercolor treatment of the same scene. Note the actual shape and proportions of the chair. The boxes stored under the table suggest the extent of the clutter in their small cottage.*

of the summer; sixty dollars worth of advance tickets were sold that night. The local reporter who attended and wrote up the event reported that Wilna and Nan's attempt to keep alive the "old Maverick spirit" had been "a huge success."[5]

In October 1960, with Wilna's memoir project faltering, and utterly unwilling to spend another winter in the Catskills, Wilna and Nan persuaded their neighbor, Ishmael Rose, to keep their bird-feeders filled and chase away marauding squirrels and then headed for Florida. If their decision to rent the cottage and move into the barn studio seems uncharacteristically rational, there was a method to their lack of madness. Wilna and Nan had now set their sights on buying a house on Anna Maria Island so that yearly winter escapes to Florida could become a permanent feature of their lifestyle. To do this, they knew they would need every cent. They also knew that essential to their achieving this dream would be winning the approval of the wealthy and influential philanthropist who had lured them to Anna Maria back in 1934, Ruth Hart Eddy. She would have to be convinced that they were being practical and responsible with their resources.

Within the world of Woodstock, Wilna and Nan's fiscal chaos and chronic shortage of funds excited little attention or concern among their friends and acquaintances. It was

Wilna Hervey, Nan and Cat at the Table. *Gouache. Nan, enjoying a glass of wine, is recognizable by the checkered jacket she wore indoors in the winter. The uninsulated cottage could be quite cool in frigid weather despite the wood-burning fireplace insert. Wilna shows a copy of* Art News *on the table.*

simply part of who they were. Most would have agreed with William Pachner's succinct and affectionate appraisal of his friends. "They were not burdened by bourgeois notions of frugality," he remembered. "They were generous, they liked to party, and they believed money was meant to be spent."[6]

Ruth Hart Eddy saw things differently, however, and over the years of paying visits to their modest cottage in Bearsville, hosting the girls at her Peru, Vermont, summer retreat and socializing with them during their winters in Florida, she grew increasingly alarmed at the financial crises that seemed to follow Wilna and Nan more faithfully than their ubiquitous dogs. A shrewd and decisive executive long used to managing large sums of money, Miss Eddy was not one to let such a situation go uncorrected forever. Therefore, at some point in the early fifties, along with her generous dollops of financial advice, Eddy began providing her Woodstock friends with a generous monthly allowance. There were strings attached, however. They had to demonstrate that they were capable of applying common sense to their personal finances, and they had to agree that they would seek her approval and advice before making major financial decisions. While the exact amount of her largesse is unknown, it is apparent that Eddy continued to send her friends a check every month until her death in 1971.[7]

The "Barn Studio." When the girls returned from Florida to their new barn residence in May 1961, they encountered a freak late-spring snowstorm. It was the last time they had to deal with snow in Bearsville. The studio apartment in the former barn would be their final home in Woodstock.

Summer costume party in Bearsville. Considering how many parties the girls hosted, it is surprising how few photos have survived. In this rare glimpse of a gathering in the fifties, guests are arriving at their cottage at the start of what is guaranteed to be a long and spirited evening of fun. Lorraine Pachner, wife of painter Bill Pachner, can be seen at left. The woman in the wig is Peggy Braun.[1]

Thus, the need to placate Ruth Eddy was ever present on their minds during the winter of 1960/61 as Wilna and Nan shopped for a house, taking an occasional break to buy and ship crates of grapefruit and other gifts to their friends in Woodstock. With the help of Robert Knowles, a local lawyer they had befriended, the snowbirds found exactly what they were looking for. There was a tiny house on Willow Avenue located only two hundred feet from the beach. It had a garage, was small enough not to be a burden and,

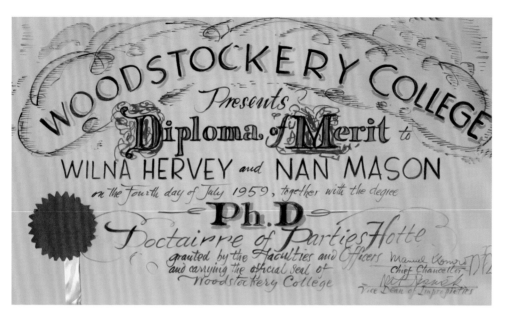

A Ph.D. from Woodstockery College. The annual summer costume picnics at Wilna and Nan's Bearsville home had, by the nineteen-fifties, become "one of the traditional highlights of the Woodstock art colony," according to the local press,[1] and were attended by upwards of a hundred people. When they outdid themselves with an extravaganza on the Fourth of July in 1959, novelist Manuel Komroff and writer/photographer Nathan Resnick honored the girls' years of effort with a Ph.D.—a "Doctairre of Parties Hotte."

best of all, had another, even smaller, house in the back that could be rented out. Taxes were low, and it was available at a bargain price.

It fell to Nan to write to their friend and patron and solicit her support for their purchase of the little bungalow. In a four-page letter addressed to "Dearest Ruth and Little Alice" and signed "Your Nannie and Willie," Nan laid out a crisp and detailed financial argument for the purchase. She calculated the rents they could apply to the mortgage, pointed out the likely appreciation that would accrue and promised that they would sell more of their Bearsville real estate to support the purchase. She also reminded her friends that, since the administration of the Hervey Post Trust had come to them following the death of Wilna's sister Eleanor, she and Wilna learned much about handling money and had made a valiant attempt to rein in their profligate ways: "You girls must know that we have learned to be practical."

In addition to the dollars and cents arguments, there were delicate and personal issues that Nan urged Ruth Eddy to consider. Wilna was having increasingly severe hip problems as a result of worsening arthritis. If they owned a house, as opposed to renting, they could install a raised toilet, high enough for Wilna to use without assistance. Such a facility had already been added to the Bearsville barn studio.[8]

In June 1961, with the blessing of Ruth Eddy, Wilna and Nan became the owners of 112 Willow Avenue on Anna Maria Island. As well as selling off another of their Bearsville properties as promised, Wilna raised cash by consigning two of her mother's old family oil portraits by the artist Chester Harding to the Rehn Gallery in Manhattan—a clear indication of how much she wanted the little bungalow near the beach.[9] The girls would spend every winter on Anna Maria for the rest of their lives.

Right, top: The Cottage on Anna Maria Island. Nan's carefully planned landscaping can be appreciated in this snapshot she took of their Florida home at 112 Willow Avenue, Anna Maria Island. The limited space around the house was filled with as many flowers and shrubs as Nan could manage to squeeze in.

Right, center: Nan Mason, Mullet Fishermen. *Wilna and Nan both loved to fish and their enthusiasm carried over into a fascination with the professional fishermen they encountered in both California and Florida. This photograph, taken by Nan, of fishermen straining to pull in their nets inspired one of Wilna's several enamels of the same subject matter.*

Below: Wilna Hervey, Beach Scene. *Enamel on copper diptych. To suggest the dazzling light reflecting off the sand, Wilna first applied a layer of gold foil to the copper tile, then baked on layers of translucent enamel. In bright light this piece literally shimmers.*

Left: Nan Mason, Wilna with Two Dogs on the Beach. *While the cats preferred to stay home, the family dogs were always more than happy to accompany the girls to the beach. Here, Wilna dries off after a swim, guarded by sentinel spaniels posted on either side.*

Below: Wilna Hervey, Shore Birds at Sunset. *Enamel. The tide has gone out and the last rays of the setting sun create a fleeting otherworldly glow on the beach where shore birds forage in the wet sand. As the focal point of this luminous image, Wilna has carefully chosen an intense reddish orange hue for the sun. To achieve sufficient saturation of color required multiple applications of enamel and repeated firing.*

Right: Nan Mason, Zebra Fish. *Enamel on copper. Nan was fascinated by tropical fish and did numerous studies of them. Several of her drawings became compositions for enamels like this. Others were used as designs for silk-screened cards that she and Wilna gave to friends as gifts.*

Below: Wilna Hervey, Egrets (a.k.a. Feeding Birds). *Enamel on copper. In a sea of lily pads, two little ducks can be seen wending their way among the big birds as they feed. One of the birds has just caught a fish, the only pop of red color that Wilna includes in the whole composition. Wilna debuted this work with the Sarasota Art Association in 1960. It was one of her favorites and was never offered for sale.*

Top left: Wilna Hervey, Barefoot Fishermen on Wharf. *Enamel on copper. Whether in California, Florida or New Jersey, any visit to the seashore was incomplete unless Wilna and Nan headed for the fishing piers to throw a line into the ocean. Wilna once let the local newspaper know they had arrived at their Anna Maria home by sending back the message "The fishing is great!"*[2]

Top right: Wilna Hervey, Anna Maria Beach Scene. *Enamel on copper. With their Florida home only two hundred feet from the beach, Wilna and Nan spent entire days under beach umbrellas enjoying the breezes and the sounds of happy children. The number of beach scenes that Wilna created speaks to her unending enjoyment of this environment.*

Left: Wilna Hervey, A Day on the Beach. *Enamel. As Wilna's hips began to fail, the task of lugging the umbrella, food, table, sketchbooks, camera and a deck of canasta cards for a day on the beach fell to Nan. Note that Wilna shows her hand on a cane as she sits facing the waves. The dog is likely one of theirs.*

"It Seems Almost Too Late"

Wilna and Nan returned to Woodstock early in the spring of 1962 to be near Eugene Speicher, whose health was rapidly failing. After Elsie Speicher died in November 1959, following several years of ill health, her husband had gone downhill steadily. During the summer of 1961 the girls had spent most of July and August helping their old friend sort through stacks of art work piled in his studio and prepare some items for shipment to the Rehn Gallery in Manhattan, where they were offered for sale. Along with the fact that many of these works had never been signed, the oil paintings needed to be stretched. Wilna and Nan handled all the details, as Speicher no longer possessed the mental focus and physical stamina to do so.

Now, in May of 1962, with the artist hailed in the thirties as America's greatest living painter fading away, there was little to do except visit and try to comfort him. Keeping vigil, Wilna stayed by Speicher's side day after day until, in the final hours of his life, he slipped into a coma. At that point, Wilna's ability to deal with her sorrow gave out. She suddenly fell sick with flu-like symptoms so severe that she was confined to her bed. Nan, too, was quite ill with a severe cold, but was unable to take to her bed, as the doctor required her to administer medications and fluids to Wilna on an hourly basis. Neither of them was able to attend Eugene Speicher's funeral on May 14th. Ten days later, just as they were beginning to recover their strength, came the unhappy news that another of their close friends, John Striebel, patriarch of Woodstock's community of cartoonists, had died. "What a miserable spring homecoming for us," Wilna lamented to John Clancy, the agent who handled Speicher's works at the Rehn Gallery.[1]

Eugene Speicher had grown extremely fond of both Wilna and Nan over the forty-plus years of their friendship. A year before his death, their mutual friend Louise Lindin had passed along to the girls an affectionate tribute he had recently paid to Wilna over dinner, extolling her "rare qualities." It is not surprising, then, that

A tale of two gardens. At both of their homes, the artists grew flowers. While the space available in Florida was limited, the Bearsville gardens tended to be huge and required a lot of work on Nan's part after Wilna began to have difficulty getting around.

Speicher's will made generous provisions for his friends. In addition to each of them receiving one of his paintings, they inherited five parcels of real estate totaling more than three acres of land near the Speicher home in Rock City. While they sold the real estate and put the money in the bank that fall, the paintings were taken to Florida and hung in the girls' winter home, where they would be prominently displayed and treasured until the end of their lives.[2]

▲ ▲ ▲

By the early sixties the lives of Wilna Hervey and Nan Mason had been dramatically transformed. Thanks to Ruth Eddy's generosity, advice and guidance, the Speicher bequest, and the sale of their remaining idle but taxable properties, they were debt-free, their finances stable, predictable and in order for the first time in decades.[3] Also, they had downsized and significantly simplified their lives. With two small homes that were easy to maintain, and with only three, then two and finally just one small pet, they were free to focus more of their energies on producing art and enjoying a somewhat sedate but still pleasant social life with a select circle of friends.

In Florida, when they weren't working in their modest studio—a glass-enclosed porch on the back of their house—their time was spent on the beach, lounging under

Flower garden at 112 Willow Avenue. Leaning on one of her canes, Wilna cuts roses from the bushes Nan planted at their Florida home.

a huge umbrella where they ate, played canasta on a portable table, enjoyed the sights and sounds of happy children, and, of course, sketched and took photographs. Scenes of beach life became a prominent motif of Wilna's enamel painting and Nan's photography. The beach visits were not all idleness, however. Both of the girls had always loved to swim and frequently took advantage of the clear blue waters of the Gulf to get some exercise. For Wilna, it was now the only physical activity not inhibited by her arthritis.

Within a short drive of their home on Anna Maria was a thriving art colony in Sarasota. There was as well an active art center at Sarasota and two others at nearby Longboat Key and Bradenton. Wilna and Nan joined all three art centers so they could exhibit their new works, take courses, and meet other artists and craftspeople. Eagerly volunteering for committees that needed help, assisting in staging social events, and always willing to regale their new friends with amusing anecdotes of the days when Wilna made her living tossing telephone poles and lifting trolley cars as Powerful Katrinka, they quickly became popular figures and minor celebrities in their new communities.

For once, Nan Mason even ventured into a significant activity without her partner; she joined the local dramatic troupe, the Island Players, on Anna Maria. While she does not seem to have appeared in any of the plays, one of her dogs did when the director just happened to have a part for a pooch. Nan designed and painted sets and posters,

helped apply makeup and even served on the board of directors for three years, starting in 1961. The plays' director, Harold Igo, and his wife became part of Nan and Wilna's social circle.[4]

Artistically, the months that the girls spent in Florida each year were now their most productive times. In Bearsville there tended to be more distractions, among them an abundance of social events, exchange of dinners with old friends, and maintenance of the huge flower gardens they continued to cultivate on their eight-acre property. In Florida, free from these obligations, they were able to concentrate on new works of art for long periods without interruption. Reflecting these realities, the bulk of the works produced by both artists in the sixties and seventies feature Florida scenes and subject matter. Showing their work in exhibitions mounted by the three art centers, both Wilna and Nan frequently won awards. From the mid-sixties on, not a year went by without one or both of them receiving some kind of recognition for their enamels, paintings or photographs. While they continued to exhibit in Woodstock and won some prizes there as well, the majority of their awards now came from shows in Florida.

For quite a while, Wilna was reluctant to do more than just show her enamel paintings to the public. When she exhibited a group of panels with the Sarasota Art Association in 1960, she marked them "not for sale." She also declined to sell when they went on view with the Woodstock Guild of Craftsmen. When her work won her a

Right: Nan Mason, Wilna Hervey. *On the occasion of Wilna's first solo enamel exhibition in Woodstock, Nan took this flattering photo to be used for publicity. In addition to appearing in several newspapers, the portrait was made into a large poster for Wilna's show.*

Left: Wilna Hervey, Picnic on the Bay. *Enamel. One of the largest and most ambitious enamels she ever created, this piece was crafted in 1969 after Wilna recovered from a broken hip. The work was shown both at the annual juried show in Bradenton, Florida, and later that year in Woodstock. She was never willing to sell it.*

Right and opposite top: Wilna Hervey: Three enamel studies of floral arrangements. Wilna and Nan kept cut flowers from their gardens in vases throughout both of their homes. In addition to the immediate enjoyment they derived from them, they photographed the bouquets, sketched them, and put all the images into albums for future reference when devising compositions for their art works. The majority of the awards Wilna won in the sixties were for floral-themed enamels.

Right: Wilna Hervey, The Large Bouquet.

Far left: Wilna Hervey, Still Life with Lillies.

Left: Wilna Hervey, Blue Vase.

Far left: Nan Mason, Calendula. Oil painting. Throughout her career, Nan had a love of still life arrangements and frequently created these indoor "landscapes" as subjects for her work. Not surprisingly, they were often centered upon bouquets of flowers.

Left: Nan Mason, Nasturtiums. One of the few enamels in which Nan used the painterly technique that Wilna favored. Despite its small size, it includes numerous delicate details such as the veins on the leaves.

Left: Wilna Hervey, Interior with Flowers on a Table, I. *As a variation on her theme of cut flowers in vases, Wilna often showed large floral arrangements displayed in intimate domestic spaces. In this view a kitchen is dominated by what appears to be a flowering shrub on the table.*

Right: Wilna Hervey, Interior with Flowers on a Table, II. *Here, the huge bouquet appears to be taller than the little girl admiring it. Wilna once told a reporter: "I'm a big woman, but I want my pictures to stay small."[1] These two pieces are the tiniest paintings Wilna did in enamels. Either would have fit comfortably in the palm of Wilna's hand.*

Wilna Hervey, The Tall Girl. *Centered on a vase of flowers, this intriguing composition is full of surprises and challenges to the viewer's perceptions. Though the remarkably tall girl seems to be arranging the flowers, she is shown standing behind the arrangement. The color of the girl's hair and the flecks of gold throughout the scene are glimpses of gold foil underlying the layers of enamel.*

scholarship from the Longboat Key Art Center in February 1964, Wilna chose to advance her enameling skills even further by studying under a local craftsperson of some repute, Hazel Ridyard. Together with Miss Ridyard, Wilna experimented with an age-old preoccupation of enamellists: the effect of heat on certain colors. Wilna's diligence paid off. At a show in April 1965, one of her new enamels won a blue ribbon. Ten months later, after winning several more awards in Florida for her work, Wilna finally dared to offer her enamels for sale.[5]

Even with all her previous accolades, Wilna was astonished when one of her pieces immediately sold for one hundred dollars to a collector, who then insisted on seeing more of her work. In the summer of 1966, Wilna's enamels were presented on exhibit and for sale at the Rudolph Galleries in Woodstock. At the age of seventy-two, Wilna was finally having her first solo exhibition. The result was overwhelming; every work on view was bought off the walls and carried away by enthusiastic gallery patrons.[6]

Always more interested in design and craftsmanship than Wilna, Nan took her enameling in a different direction. Using sunflowers or seagulls—the latter a source of fascination for both her and Wilna—as motifs, Nan began to create decorative mirrors surrounded by borders of small enamel tiles. The first of her "mirror birdscapes" won her an award in 1964, inspiring her to create several more. When Nan won a significant enameling award in an early spring show in 1968, the Woodstock painter Andrée Ruellan, who well understood the dynamics of the relationship between her two friends, was quick to offer warm congratulations: "You deserve many honors, and you should feel encouraged. And when there are two artists in a family, it's nice to alternate, no?"[7] Nan would finally get her first solo exhibition in the fall of 1969, at the age of seventy-three, when her enamels were displayed at the annual craft show sponsored by the Woodstock Guild of Craftsmen.

In the fall of 1967 an enamel of a floral arrangement won Wilna the prestigious Konrad Cramer Memorial Award at the annual craft exhibition in Woodstock. "Her extraordinary skill with this medium is well demonstrated in this picture," a reviewer wrote, "and in two others in which lush flowers bloom in rich enamel reds, or glow whitely against intense depths of blue."[8] Flowers and floral arrangements were a favorite artistic theme for both Wilna and Nan. Enthusiastic gardeners all their lives, they constantly photographed their gardens and carefully placed the pictures in albums for future reference. When Nan began taking 8mm home movies in the late sixties, she devoted an entire reel to the flowers at their Bearsville home. Despite the relentless foraging of cats, their homes were never without cut flower arrangements, and these often became the subject of paintings and enamels.

The remarkable success of Wilna's show at the Rudolph Galleries brought a request for an interview from a local reporter eager to learn more about this "new art form" and share it with the public. Taking the reporter from the *Woodstock Record Press* on a tour of her Bearsville studio and home in October 1966, Wilna described her process and showed off samples of her work, including some of the early pieces that hadn't turned out so well. During the tour, Wilna, with her usual candor, revealed that even with her

Nan Mason, Wilna in a Wheelchair. *During Wilna's convalescence from her broken hip, Nan positioned her at the large kitchen window in Bearsville and then quickly sketched this view of her watching the birds.*

success in finally finding her artistic niche, her happiness was tinged with regret. "I wish I could have discovered this sooner," she mused wistfully. "I wish I had 20 years . . . it seems almost too late."[9] Though the reporter was too kind to mention it in her article, Wilna was moving slowly and leaning heavily on two canes as she recounted the evolution of her enamel paintings.

Wilna Hervey's height and weight, which had been such psychological burdens to her as a child, became serious physical liabilities to her as an aging adult. Throughout the nineteen-sixties, as Wilna was winning awards and recognition for her enamel paintings, her ability to get around and perform even simple tasks was steadily being compromised by painfully deteriorating hip joints. By the mid-sixties, Wilna was forced to rely on a cane for stability and support, and soon two canes became necessary. Two months after

Nan and Wilna with Hazel Schoeps. Both caretaker and friend to Wilna and Nan, Hazel Schoeps poses with them on the beach near their home on Anna Maria Island. Without Hazel's help, Wilna might not have recovered from her broken hip and the girls certainly would not have been able to continue their yearly trips between Woodstock and Florida. Hazel was the last of the Big Girls' "adopted daughters."

she won the Cramer Award, in the fall of 1967, one of her fragile hips was fractured in a fall. Dr. Norman Berg, the Woodstock physician who treated the incapacitated artist as she lay confined to her bed for two months, could see that she was going to need more short-term care and long-term rehabilitation than Nan could provide. He recommended they contact another of his patients whom he thought would make a good caretaker. Her name was Hazel Schoeps.[10]

Hazel Schoeps's original role in the lives of Wilna and Nan was that of personal health assistant, helping with personal hygiene, bathing Wilna in her bed and coaxing her through stretching exercises after the hip had begun to heal. As time went on, however, Hazel's role expanded, partly out of necessity and partly out of a growing fondness for her eccentric and endearing clients. An outgoing, down-to-earth woman with no pretensions, she fit into their world and enjoyed their company as much as they enjoyed hers. Hazel became an indispensable part of their lives, and a close friend to Wilna and Nan from 1968 until their deaths.

After Wilna's fracture, the annual retreat to Anna Maria would have been impossible without Hazel Schoeps. Apart from the physical difficulties of travel, Wilna's disability made it hard for her to pack the hundreds of unnecessary items she insisted she couldn't live without no matter where she lived. Though the details of what she packed and shipped each season are not clear, it does appear that the dozens of boxes contained more than just clothing, personal belongings and household goods. Each November,

Far left: Wilna on the beach in Anna Maria. By the early seventies Wilna could reach the beach two hundred feet from her home only by walking slowly and carefully, supported by her two canes. Once there, she looked forward to going in for a swim. It was now the only exercise she could get.

Left: Wilna swimming. Once in the water, Wilna could get around much better than she could on dry land. Weather permitting, she always celebrated New Year's Day by taking a plunge in the warm waters of the Gulf of Mexico near her Anna Maria beach home.

Hazel helped them pack and send the boxes, then traveled with them and their final pet—a very indulged Siamese cat—on the train to Florida. There she spent two weeks helping them open up their house, unpack, shop for groceries and get settled in before returning to Woodstock. In the spring, Hazel went back to Florida, helped them pack and close up the house and rode with them on the train to New York. During the months in Florida when Hazel wasn't around, the girls contracted the services of local nurses.[11]

After her fracture, Wilna's love of swimming took on greater importance, as it was now the only exercise she was capable of. Painfully making her way the two hundred feet to the beach, on two canes and with Nan's help, Wilna would ease into the waves. Then, with her natural buoyancy to assist her, the powerful swimmer Wilna always was would return and she would swim long laps like an Olympian, doing breaststrokes and backstrokes in the clear blue water. In one of Nan's home movies, a younger gay couple the girls had met at one of the art centers are seen teaching Wilna how to snorkel. After Frankie and George, who had met in the Navy some years before, adjust her face mask and show her how to use the breathing tube, they gently lead her into the water, one on each side to support her. Then Wilna takes off, face down, enjoying a new adventure with her characteristic enthusiasm. Later, as she floats on her back without the mask, beaming like a happy child, it is hard to believe she has so many physical ailments. Small wonder that Wilna told the local newspapers she felt better on Anna Maria than anywhere else.[12]

▲ ▲ ▲

On two occasions in their lives, Wilna and Nan were asked to pose together for Wood-stock artists. In the fall of 1927, after returning from their long European adventure, they were the subjects of a photographic study by Alfred Cohn. Wearing neckties under their winter coats and sporting the jaunty berets in fashion in Woodstock at that time, the two smiling young artists stood close together as equal partners ready to face their future together.

The second time they posed came forty-two years later, in the studio of their friend the Woodstock painter Franklin Alexander. The girls had known Alexander since 1955. In the fifties, chastened by the fact that Ruth Eddy was supplementing their income, and heeding her admonitions, Wilna had actually gotten a job of sorts, obtaining a real estate license and dabbling in the sale of properties. When Frank-lin Alexander and his wife, Pia Oste Alexander, came to Woodstock looking for a home, it was Wilna who sold them their house. She also welcomed the two artists to Woodstock in the best possible way. She invited them to a huge summer party so they could meet a rich and eclectic assortment of painters, cartoonists, ceramicists and writers, such as the novelist and screenwriter Manuel Komroff, who wore a red wig and a flashing electric bowtie for the occasion. Also in attendance were Dr. Joseph Shakuri Tomas, the Iraqi spokesman for the Arab League, the internationally famous collector and singer of folksongs Sam Eskin, Wilna's nephew Bruce Cator, who had been a bomber pilot during the war, and several victims of Hiroshima who were being treated by Dr. Hitzig.[13]

Working in oils in the summer of 1969, Franklin Alexander captured both the physical and the psychological changes that had reshaped the two longtime compan-ions and redefined their relationship over the decades. Wilna sits in a large wooden chair, filling it to capacity, facing the viewer, who cannot help but be impressed by her monumental presence. She is tastefully attired, perhaps wearing one of the outfits made for her by the seamstress Clara Russell of nearby West Hurley, who crafted all of Wilna's outsized fashionable clothes in those days.[14] There has been no attempt to flatter her, nor has the artist exaggerated her features. Approaching her seventy-fifth birthday and suffering from numerous maladies, she is as she is. Nan, also fashionably dressed—in purple—and wearing jewelry, is shown in profile, off to the side and seated slightly back, facing the space just behind Wilna. Her position in the composition serves to focus our attention on Wilna and even magnify her size. From her vantage point, and with what appears to be a slightly lifted eyebrow, Nan can keep an eye on her partner of forty-five years without intruding into her space. Wilna is the center of Nan's world and Nan is content, as she has been all her adult life, to let Wilna shine on center stage while she takes her place in a supporting role. Even Nan's choice of attire says much, in that the color purple is considered symbolic of spiritual bonding and loving support. It is obvious that Franklin Alexander knew his friends well and understood the dynamics of their relationship.

Wilna Hervey,
Underwater.
*Enamel. One of the
last known enamel
paintings Wilna
made, this piece was
the direct result of
her learning how to
snorkel in the Gulf
waters near her
Florida home. Wilna
gave this work to
two of her Woodstock
friends, the artists
Andrée Ruellan and
Jack Taylor.*

CHAPTER 18

Shadows on the Sand

I n 1971 Wilna Hervey and Nan Mason lost three lifelong friends in the span of six months. Molly Pollock, Wilna's first and only friend from her youth, died in May, followed only weeks later by Ruth Hart Eddy, in June. Miss Eddy had been living alone in Vermont, in failing health, since her companion, Alice Gilman, had died in 1967. At the end of November word came to them in Florida that Maud Petersham, by then a widow, had died as well. A few weeks before Christmas, sobered by their losses and confronted with increasingly frequent reminders of their own mortality, Wilna and Nan went out to their beach at sunset so Nan could take a poignant photograph of their lengthening shadows on the sand. It was a poetic metaphor for two old artists approaching the end of their days. Wilna included a copy of the photo in each Christmas card she sent that year.[1]

Ruth Eddy's passing, at age eighty-six, brought Wilna and Nan a final measure of financial security. Intent on continuing the monetary support she had provided her friends for many years, Miss Eddy set aside for them the sum of two hundred thousand dollars in trust. The money was to be invested, and the girls were to receive five percent of the fair market value of the trust each year, with no distinction being drawn between principal and income. Miss Eddy's generous bequest to Wilna and Nan was the largest of several trusts she set up to benefit old friends and family members, a measure of her affection for the only other same-sex couple she and Alice Gilman had known in all their years together. It was, as well, a measure of her understanding that her friends would need her help even more in the years ahead. In her final gesture of friendship, Ruth Hart Eddy, the administrator of a foundation devoted to the health concerns of senior citizens, ensured that Wilna and Nan would be able to afford the comfort and medical care they needed in the last years of their lives.[2]

As Wilna became increasingly ill, and keenly aware that time was running out, she devoted more energy than ever to her enamel paintings, working almost obsessively at times, to the point of exhausting herself. Andrée Ruellan gently urged Wilna to take a more balanced approach to life and work. "Perhaps you have been working too hard, Willie?" she wrote in April 1972. "Of course I can understand your reluctance to stop

*Nan Mason, *Shadows on the Sand. *This poignant image, taken on the beach at Anna Maria at sunset, was inspired by the loss of three close friends months earlier. Wilna included a copy of the photo in each Christmas card she sent that year.*

Wilna Hervey, Picnic by the Lake. *Enamel. Created when Wilna was approaching her eightieth birthday, the work has two signatures, one of which is barely legible. The frothy explosions of color that make up much of this work border on the abstract and suggest that Wilna's failing eyesight may have occasioned a new approach to applying her enamels.*

work on your enamels . . . But you must not get ill—that would be disastrous! You seem to have accomplished quite a lot; and if you stay well, may be able to have a productive summer, too."[3]

By the spring of 1976 both Wilna and Nan—pushing eighty-two and eighty, respectively—were becoming feeble. Although she continued to painfully make her way to the beach on her canes, Wilna could no longer risk going in for a swim. Her eyesight was now deteriorating rapidly, a possible consequence of her advancing diabetes. In addition to the multiple illnesses she had endured for years, she had recently required an operation for skin cancer. For her part, Nan had now developed arthritis in her hips and feet, making walking painful. She had just had cataract surgery, was experiencing pain in her eyes and was also developing heart problems. Mindful that each season they spent on Anna Maria could be the last for one or both of them, Wilna and Nan decided to throw a party before they left town. When Hazel Schoeps arrived from Woodstock to assist in packing and transporting her two elderly charges back to Bearsville, they solicited her help. On the Saturday night before Easter 1976 the girls opened their home to their neighbors and their friends from the various art centers. Drinks in hand, the two geriatric party animals welcomed their guests with their customary enthusiasm.[4]

Although Wilna continued to create enamel paintings until 1978, her last known extant works are a couple of panels done in Florida in 1974 and 1975. These last efforts have more impressionistic touches than previous pieces, possibly as a result of her failing eyesight. Nan continued to produce as well, and both continued to show their work, though these final pieces were always marked "N.F.S." (not for sale). The final showing for the two enamelists was a major exhibition in Sarasota in the spring of 1978. Their enamels were not only accepted for inclusion but placed in prime locations within the show. Both octogenarian artists attended the grand opening.[5] It was the last exhibition that Wilna and Nan would attend together as well as the final public showing of their work.

By early 1978 Wilna's memory was failing as well. She wrote several times to ask friends questions they had just answered in previous letters. Her eyesight was so bad that she had to give up reading completely, a huge disappointment for a voracious reader with books quite literally stacked to the ceiling in their bedroom. When Wilna agreed (after much coaxing by Nan and Hazel) to forgo the long and exhausting train ride back to New York in late spring 1978 and fly instead, she was unable to enjoy the view from the plane. Wilna's poor eyesight was likely the reason why one of her last enamels self-destructed in the kiln during firing, ruining a week's worth of painstaking and tedious work. She apparently had failed to notice that the enamel paste had not completely dried before she fired the piece. The moisture became steam and the medium exploded, splattering her careful work all over the inside of the kiln. This episode, in April 1978, seems to have marked the end of Wilna Hervey's artistic career.[6]

In her last year, Wilna was often an invalid, spending months on end in bed at home and finally in the hospital. She is said to have become demanding and even more childlike in her final days. On March 6th, 1979, Wilna Hervey died in Manatee

Wilna Hervey, Playing on the Beach. *Enamel. The overall soft diffused effect, with people blending into each other and dissolving into the sand, adds a dream-like quality to this evocation of a bright, warm day on a Florida beach.*

Wilna Hervey, Self-Portrait in the Shower. *With arthritis crippling her fingers and her eyesight failing, Wilna often reverted to a casual technique she had improvised years before of using a ballpoint pen to scribble her drawings. This quick sketch of herself in the shower suggests that time did not diminish her sense of humor.*

Memorial Hospital in Bradenton, Florida. Though she had stayed by Wilna's side as much as possible, Nan wasn't with her at the end. She had just returned to their home to freshen up and rest when she got the call from the hospital that Wilna was gone.[7]

A number of newspapers in Florida and New York paid tribute to Wilna Hervey, all of them remembering her as "Powerful Katrinka." When Nan returned to Bearsville a few months later, she brought Wilna's ashes and had them laid to rest in the Woodstock Artists Cemetery. At the graveside service on June 3rd, conducted by the pastor of the Dutch Reformed Church, Dorothy Varian gave the eulogy. Sharing memories of their fifty-year friendship, she paid tribute to Wilna's irrepressible spirit: "Wilna was never blasé about anything—a childlike joy and eagerness was her essence."[8] When Frank Capra learned of Wilna's death, he wrote feelingly of the actress he had described in his 1971 memoirs as "that wonderful sweet giant." "I share your sorrow for the loss of our great big-hearted friend, Wilna," he wrote to Nan. "But the sorrows, God willing, will soon give way to the lovely, happy memories that you must have acquired from a most loyal friend during the 59 years that you were together."[9]

In her last will and testament, Wilna left her entire estate to her "friend of years," Nan Mason. But the will also designated dozens of bequests in the event that Nan did not survive her.[10] Nan, ever loyal and sensitive to Wilna's wishes, gave several art works to longtime friends, as Wilna would have wanted, and transferred some of Wilna's other wishes to her own will.

Some time after Wilna's funeral, the Pachners invited Nan to dinner. She arrived at their house, where she had once supervised construction and designed gardens, dressed in widow's black. Bill Pachner recalled that "it was eerie" to see her without Wilna. After dinner, the artist took Nan to his studio to show her his latest works. He had by now told her that he was losing the sight in his one good eye and would soon be blind. As Nan stepped forward to look at the paintings, she reached into a pocket and took out a handkerchief. Standing alone in the Pachner studio for the first time without Wilna, contemplating the fact that the wonderful paintings she saw before her would soon be unseen by their creator, Nan was overwhelmed. Pachner stood back quietly watching her as she wept.[11]

Nan Mason was not one to dwell on the past, however. Despite her grief and loneliness, she remained optimistic and forward-looking. Though now quite frail, she continued with her routines. With Hazel's help, she still shuttled seasonally between Bearsville and Anna Maria, occasionally venturing out to exhibitions and shows. Though she made no more enamels, she continued to draw, and even made an improvement to her Willow Avenue cottage. Not interested in sitting on the beach alone, she added a screen porch

Nan and Wilna in their garden in Bearsville. Taken just before they left for Florida in the fall of 1977, it is one of the last photos of the girls together. Wilna is noticeably thinner and would spend much of the next year and a half in bed.

where she and her cat could enjoy the ocean breezes. Friends who dropped in to see her in Florida or at the studio barn in Bearsville found Nan as eager as ever to hear all about their lives. She still liked to go out to dinner, have a drink or two and giggle over nothing in particular as she always had. She did not want to reminisce.

It had always been the girls' policy to put their valuable art in storage when they left one home for another. While some lesser pieces might remain on the walls of either residence, the valuable paintings, in particular works by Eugene Speicher, were taken down and transferred to the Kingston Transfer Company in Kingston, New York, or to a storage facility in Bradenton, Florida. Besides their considerable value, the Speicher paintings and drawings held great emotional resonance for his old friends.

In the spring of 1981 Hazel helped Nan put her art collection in storage before leaving Anna Maria for the flight back to New York. It was the last time Nan would see her beloved paintings. When she and Hazel returned to Florida in the fall, they found the storage unit empty. During her absence, Nan's lawyer, Robert Knowles, had used his power of attorney to access the vault, take the art and sell it. What reasons he gave her are unknown. Knowles was by all accounts a very persuasive man, a garrulous and successful politician. He must have told Nan that the sale was, somehow, in her best interests. Though devastated by the loss of her art, Nan either accepted his explanation or was too confused and tired, at the age of eighty-five and suffering from heart disease, to fight back. Despite this shock, she agreed to sign a new will that Knowles prepared for her three months later, a will that gave him complete power over the disposition of her estate. Had she known the rest of the story, she might have had second thoughts about signing anything. Unknown to his clients, Knowles was an alcoholic who had for some time been systematically removing funds from Nan's account, and those of three other elderly women, and depositing the money in his own accounts.[12]

Nan would never be aware of this final betrayal. She died only five weeks after signing her new will. In early March a young friend from Woodstock, Peggy Laughner, was visiting Nan and looking after her. On the morning of March 2nd, when Nan failed to appear for breakfast, her visitor went to check on her and found Nan dead; her heart had given out while she slept. "[A]n overnight blow to us all," Dorothy Varian lamented, "for dearest Nan gave such healthy assurance of living, laughing and playing forever."[13]

Nan's will directed that the house on Anna Maria Island go to Hazel Schoeps. Her home in Bearsville went to Andrée Ruellan and her husband, Jack Taylor. All of the art Nan had placed in storage in Kingston—safe from the depredations of her Florida lawyer—went to the Woodstock Artists Association. In all, thirty-three paintings, drawings, collages, lithographs and prints by sixteen Woodstock artists were included in this bequest. Eight friends received financial gifts, the largest going to Peggy Laughner, who was with Nan at the end. There was also a gift of five hundred dollars to the North Shore Animal League in Port Washington, Long Island, a pioneer in the no-kill shelter movement and the source of many of the girls' endless procession of pets over the years. Nan's biggest bequest—thirty thousand dollars—went to the Eddy

Nan Mason, Ebb-Tide. *Looking out over the Gulf of Mexico from the beach near their Anna Maria home, Nan took this photograph of the setting sun. The rocks in the foreground serve to anchor this view in the physical world while the display of light and shadow in the heavens speaks of a more spiritual dimension.*

Foundation at Samaritan Hospital in Troy, New York, with the notation, "in honor and respect and out of love and appreciation for my dear friend, Ruth Hart Eddy." It was only because of Ruth Eddy that Nan and Wilna had that kind of money in their accounts at the end of their lives.[14]

On Sunday, June 6th, 1982, Nan Mason's ashes were interred in Woodstock in an afternoon graveside service that mirrored Wilna's interment three summers earlier. Once again called upon to offer a eulogy, Dorothy Varian gave a brief but heartfelt tribute, concluding with a statement that reflected the sentiments of the dwindling circle of old friends standing by the grave: "What a gift of friendship and fun it was to have known Nan Mason and Wilna Hervey for fifty or more long years."[15]

Beneath small identical headstones marked only with their names and dates and the word "Artist," Wilna and Nan rest side by side in the Woodstock Artists Cemetery. In death, as in life, they are surrounded by a multitude of friends.

The Legacy of Wilna Hervey and Nan Mason

Wilna Hervey once demonstrated the durability of her enamel paintings by pounding on one with her fist. "They're practically indestructible!" she announced to the startled reporter watching this athletic display. "I want them to last!"

And so they have, in goodly numbers, all as bright and colorful as the day they emerged from the kiln. Along with a handful of Wilna's films, a healthy sampling of Nan's enamels, and the numerous oil paintings, watercolors, prints, charcoal sketches and ink drawings done by both women, they constitute the most tangible legacy of Wilna and Nan. But the charming art works, today held by museums, archives, galleries and private collectors alike, constitute another, less obvious, legacy. Like snapshots or diary entries, they preserve the memories of places and events cherished by their makers: a warm day on a Florida beach with a breeze blowing in from the ocean; a morning when the winter sunlight falling on a bowl of pears demands that the fruit be painted before it is eaten; the neighbor's daughter playing with the cats; barefoot fishermen on the piers of Carmel pulling in their nets. The art of Wilna Hervey and Nan Mason is a tangible record of their responses to special moments in their lives.

In the fifty-nine years they spent together, Wilna and Nan went through many changes. They were actresses, artists, clowns, gourmands, musicians, dog breeders and raconteurs. They were real estate speculators and candle makers, erstwhile farmers and house painters, landscapers and party planners. But their long partnership was defined not only by the remarkable variety of things they accomplished—or were at least willing to attempt—but also by the unquenchable enthusiasm they both showed for all of it.

Fifty years and counting. At home in their art-filled cottage on Anna Maria Island, Wilna and Nan enjoy a special moment together. After more than half a century, their continued delight in each other's company is obvious.

The "childlike joy and eagerness" that Dorothy Varian declared to be Wilna's "essence" found a sympathetic vibration in Nan's makeup early on in their acquaintanceship. Ever in sympathy with her co-conspirator's endless schemes and mercurial aspirations, Nan shared Wilna's passion for the many vocations and avocations they explored in tandem. To each and every new endeavor, whether it was raising money for the Woodstock Library, constructing a doghouse that looked just like their cottage or driving across the continent in pursuit of a dream—all enterprises they tackled together—the Big Girls of Bearsville brought a generous measure of eagerness and enthusiasm. Neither one of them was ever indifferent to anything, and, conversely, neither one of them was likely to do anything for very long if she didn't really enjoy it.

Their greatest enjoyment was each other's company. To their many friends and acquaintances, their steadfast devotion as a couple was as much a part of their identity as the quaint and witty songs they sang or the wild moonlit parties they threw. Never apart from the fall of 1923 until Wilna's death in the spring of 1979, the two women inspired, encouraged, assisted, teased, protected, comforted, amused and loved each other with the same enthusiasm that they brought to bear in all aspects of their lives.

It is in their enthusiasm, their eagerness to explore the adventures that each new day might bring—and their joy in sharing them with each other—that the most important legacy of Wilna Hervey and Nan Mason is to be found. Their enduring companionship serves to remind us of a profound and timeless truth: enthusiasm and love are the secrets to a happy life, and the essence of Living Large.

Endnotes

Hervey-Mason Papers (HMP) refers to the Wilna Hervey and Nan Mason Collection at the Smithsonian's Archives of American Art in Washington, D.C.

All news items from the *Kingston Daily Freeman* and other New York-based newspapers were obtained via the Old New York State Historical Newspapers database at http://www.fultonhistory.com/Fulton.html.

Chapter 1

1 Wilna Hervey, *The Original Katrinka*, unpublished typescript, 3, Hervey-Mason Papers (HMP), box 11, folder 1.

2 Ibid.

3 Ibid.; Eva van Rijn, telephone interview with author, 12 November 2011. Wilna had related this story about her mother to Ms. van Rijn, a Woodstock artist, during a conversation in the late sixties.

4 "Brewster Riches Brought Only Woe, Wife Says," *Oakland Tribune*, 12 December 1922, B16; "Mortgage for $50,000,000 Filed," *New York Daily Tribune*, 30 May 1903, 2. Anna Hervey's first husband was Thomas V. Cator Sr., a volatile and colorful man who had once run for Senator from California on the Populist ticket and who was arrested for attacking Wilna's father with a drawn pistol in 1895; "Thomas V. Cator Draws a Pistol," *Morning Call* (San Francisco), 4 March 1895, 3; *New York, State Census*, 1915, database online: Ancestry.com.

5 "Two Kindred Spirits Discard Traditions," *Brooklyn Daily Eagle*, 16 November 1911, 6. Wilna's sister Marie also befriended Molly and they wrote a song together. In her memoir, Wilna's version of their meeting was slightly different from the newspaper account.

6 Ibid.

7 Hervey, *The Original Katrinka*, 12.

Chapter 2

1 Hal Garrott, "People Talked About," *Carmel Pine Cone*, 14 March 1930, 9.

2 Wilna Hervey, unpaginated handwritten notes for *The Original Katrinka*, HMP, box 11, folder 2; Alexandrina Robertson Harris's portrait of Professor Whittaker is at the Smithsonian American Art Museum; *The Oracle*, 1915, 64, Ancestry.com. *U.S. School Yearbooks* [database online], Provo, Utah: Ancestry.com Operations, Inc., 2010.

3 "E. V. Brewster and Miss Eleanor Cator Wed On Dec. 27," *New York Times*, 4 January 1917, 11.

4 Wilna also used the surname Wilde on the two articles she wrote. See Wilna Wilde, "Thomas Meighan, Hero of Many Fires," *Motion Picture Magazine*, 13, 1 (February), 1917, 111–113; Wilna Wilde, "Inside the Flickerville Bungalows," *Motion Picture Magazine*, 4, 3 (May), 1917, 37–40.

5 "Greenroom Jottings," *Motion Picture Classic*, 4, 3, May 1917, 58; Hervey, *The Original Katrinka*, 2–4, 9–11. Judging by her description of the film and her costume, Wilna seems to have appeared in Dooley's *Hearts and Arts*, a short comedy that also marked the screen debut of the noted silent film actress Nita Naldi.

Chapter 3

1 Hervey, *The Original Katrinka*, 7.

2 Ibid.

3 Ibid.

4 W. Tjark Reiss, "My Father Winold Reiss—Recollections by Tjark Reiss," *Queen City Heritage* (Cincinnati Historical Society), 51, 2–3, 1993, 64; *Mind and Body: A Monthly Journal Devoted to Physical Education* (Freidenker Publishing, Milwaukee), 14, 161 (September), 1907, 170.

5 Hervey, unpaginated handwritten notes.

6 Ibid.; Hervey, *The Original Katrinka*, 18.

7 Hervey, *The Original Katrinka*, 18.

8 Hervey, unpaginated handwritten notes; Wilna Hervey and Nan Mason interview with the Woodstock writer and historian Jean Gaede, 1974, cassette recording. Woodstock Artists Association and Museum (WAAM), Woodstock, N.Y.; Alf Evers, *Woodstock: History of an American Town* (Woodstock and New York: Overlook Press, Peter Mayer Publishers, 1987), 478.

9 Renate Reiss, e-mail to author, 10 September 2007. Renate Reiss, widow of Winold Reiss's son, Tjark, and archivist of the Reiss Partnership/Reiss Archives, quotes a letter from Winold Reiss to the effect that, while traveling in Germany in 1922, he had visited Bubi Schaeffer and delivered the kiss that Wilna had sent along for her friend.

10 Hervey, *The Original Katrinka*, 19.

11 Ibid., 20.

12 Wilna Hervey, untitled memoir supplement "C" typescript, 1, HMP, box 11, folder 3.

Chapter 4

1 Hervey, *The Original Katrinka*, 21.

2 Hervey, *The Original Katrinka*, 23; letter from Wilna Hervey to Roswell L. "Bob" Thompson, 14 October 1919, HMP, box 10, folder 1.

3 Hervey, *The Original Katrinka*, 27.

4 Millicent Page was appearing under the professional name Minnie LaForte when she met Dan Mason. Upon their marriage, she reverted to her maiden name.

5 *Edison Kinetogram*, 10, 7, 1 May 1914, 2; "Dan Mason, Famous Syracuse Actor, Dies at Home on Hudson," *Syracuse Journal*, 6 July 1929, 3; Dan Mason biography and filmography, Internet Movie Database: http://www.imdb.com/name/nm0556658/.

6 Hervey, *The Original Katrinka*, 27–30.

7 Ibid., 30.

Chapter 5

1 Ibid., 30, 31.

2 Ibid., 35.

3 Ibid., 36.

4 Hervey, untitled memoir supplement "J" typescript, 2, HMP, box 11, folder 3.; Census of the United States, 1900, 1910, 1920, online versions at Ancestry.com; letters from Dan Mason to Nan Mason, 14 October 1924, 16 February 1926, HMP, box 4, folder 2.

5 Deed of sale from Theodore Lane Bean et ux. to Daniel G. Mason, 5 May 1920, Montgomery County, Pa., Deed Book 807, 431–432, Montgomery County Recorder of Deeds, Norristown, Pa.; Hervey, *The Original Katrinka*, 41, 42.

6 Hervey, *The Original Katrinka*, 61.

7 Ibid., 42.

8 Ibid., 27; letter from Nan Mason to Wilna Hervey, 30 October 1920, and other, undated letters from 1920, HMP, box 4, folder 5.

9 Wilna Hervey, untitled memoir supplement "B," 3–6, HMP, box 11, folder 3.

10 Letter from Nan Mason to Wilna Hervey, 22 November 1920, HMP, box 4, folder 5.

11 Letter from Nan Mason to Wilna Hervey, 17 December 1920, HMP, box 4, folder 5.

12 Letter from Nan Mason to Wilna Hervey, 18 December 1920, HMP, box 4, folder 5.

13 *The Arts: A Journal Appearing Every Month During the Arts Season* (Hamilton Easter Field, Editor and Publisher, Brooklyn, N.Y.), 1, no 2 (January), 1921, 58.

14 Hervey, unpaginated handwritten notes.

15 Hervey, *The Original Katrinka*, 61.

16 Ibid.

17 Ibid.; Hervey, unpaginated handwritten notes; letter from Anna Hervey to Nan Mason, 25 April 1921, HMP, box 2, folder 7.

18 Letter from Nan Mason to Wilna Hervey, 30 October 1920, HMP, box 4, folder 5; deed of sale from Emaretta Lasher to Wilna Hervey, 11 November 1920. Ulster County, N.Y., Deed Book 479, 27–28, Ulster County Clerk's Office, Kingston, N.Y.

19 Her trainer was Lawson Robertson, brother of her friend and former teacher Alexandrina Robertson Harris. Robertson was a former Olympic trainer and was in Philadelphia serving as coach for the University of Pennsylvania's track team; Hervey, *The Original Katrinka*, 30; Hervey, memoir supplement "B," 4.

20 Hervey, *The Original Katrinka*, 62.

Chapter 6

1 Ibid.; letter from Dan Mason to Wilna Hervey, 26 September 1921, HMP, box 3, folder 10.

2 Deed of sale from Grace H. Britton to Wilna Hervey, 29 September 1921. Ulster County, N.Y., Deed Book 485, 163–164, Ulster County Clerk's Office, Kingston, N.Y.; Hervey, *The Original Katrinka*, 62.

3 Telegram from Dan Mason to Wilna Hervey, n.d., c. January 1922. Daniel Gelfand Collection, Woodstock, N.Y.; Wilna Hervey, contract with Paul Gerson Pictures Corporation, 9 February 1922, HMP, box 11, folder 7.

4 Hervey, memoir supplement "J," 1; postcard from Wilna Hervey to Winold Reiss, May or June 1922, Reiss Archives. The author wishes to thank Robert Birchard for making available his copy of *Pop Tuttle's Movie Queen* for study purposes.

5 Anna V. H. T. Hervey, Last Will and Testament, 27 December 1920, Queens County, N.Y. Recorded in Wills of Real Estate, Book 114, 307,

18 April 1922, Surrogate's Court, Jamaica, N.Y.; "E.V. Brewster Named in Mystery Suit by His Second Wife," *Brooklyn Daily Eagle*, 25 March 1922, 1. According to calculations using the Web site *Measuring Worth* (http://www. measuringworth.com/uscompare/), Wilna's inheritance from her mother would be approximately $6.5 million in today's money.

6 Hervey, memoir supplement: "CALIFORNIA" typescript, 2, HMP, box 11, folder 3; Hervey, memoir supplement "J," 5; Hervey, memoir supplement "Incidents—California," unpaginated typescript, HMP, box 11, folder 3.

7 Hervey, *The Original Katrinka*, 70.

8 Ibid., 71; Frank Capra, *The Name Above the Title: An Autobiography* (New York: Macmillan, 1971), 35.

9 Hervey, *CALIFORNIA*, 4; postcard from Wilna Hervey to Winold Reiss, 1922.

10 Bernice Birkman, "Former Star of Those Toonerville Trolley Comedies Lives on Island," *Bradenton Herald*, 24 March 1965; unpaginated clipping, Wilna Hervey file, WAAM.

11 "Flashes from Frisco," *Camera Magazine* 5, no 42, 1923, 20; deed of sale from Carmel Development Company to Wilna Hervey, 25 January 1923, Monterey County, Calif., Deed Book 2, 320, Monterey County Recorder, Salinas, Calif.; postcard from Wilna Hervey to Winold Reiss, 1922.

12 Letter from Dan Mason to Wilna Hervey (from Los Angeles), 14 June 1923, HMP, box 3, folder 10.

13 Deed of sale from Emaretta Lasher to Wilna Hervey, 16 May 1923, Ulster County, N.Y., Deed Book 505, 106, Ulster County Clerk's Office, Kingston, N.Y.

14 Wilna Hervey, chronology for *The Original Katrinka*, unpaginated typescript, HMP, box 11, folder 1.

CHAPTER 7

1 Letter from Eleanor Brewster to Wilna Hervey, 12 March 1924, HMP, box 1, folder 12.

2 Letter from Dan Mason to Nan Mason and Wilna Hervey, 14 June 1924, HMP, box 3, folder 11.

3 Richard H. Love, *Carl W. Peters: American Scene Painter from Rochester to Rockport* (Rochester, N.Y.: University of Rochester Press, 1999), 217. Louise Johnson, in a letter to the editor of the *Miami Daily News* in 1940, pointed out that the term "Blue Dome Fellowship" actually derived from Dewing Woodward's favorite expression, "Worship God under the Blue Dome of Heaven"; see "Here's What People Have to Say: The Blue Dome Fellowship," *Miami Daily News*, 29 December 1940, 10-A; Pat Horner, "The Blue Dome Fraternity—a Niche in Cre-

ation," http://woodstockguide.com/musings. html#bluedome (19 March 2014).

4 "Blue Dome in Miami," *Kingston Daily Freeman*, 4 August 1919, 9; "Reforesting Ulster Land," *Kingston Daily Freeman*, 11 February 1922, 7.

5 "Large Crowd at the Maverick," *Kingston Daily Freeman*, 15 August 1924, 10; "The Maverick Festival, Woodstock, 1915–1931," online exhibition at http://www.newpaltz.edu/museum/exhibitions/maverick/index.htm; Wilna Hervey and Nan Mason interview with Jean Gaede.

6 Letter from Dan Mason to Wilna Hervey and Nan Mason, 9 October 1924, HMP, box 3, folder 11; deed of sale from John P. Lasher to Nan L. Grassman Mason, 3 October 1924, Ulster County, N.Y., Deed Book 506, 398, Ulster County Clerk's Office, Kingston, N.Y.; deed of sale from Fred Shultis and Lottie Shultis to Wilna Hervey, 20 June 1924, Ulster County, N.Y., Deed Book 506, 187; deed of sale from Emaretta Lasher to Wilna Hervey, 12 September 1924, Ulster County, N.Y., Deed Book 506, 415, Ulster County Clerk's Office, Kingston, N.Y.; deed of sale from Paul A. Carley and Ruth V. Carley to Wilna Hervey, 4 October 1924, Ulster County, N.Y., Deed Book 506, 503, Ulster County Clerk's Office, Kingston, N.Y.

CHAPTER 8

1 New York State Census for Town of Woodstock, Ulster County, 1 June 1925, online version at Ancestry.com; Hervey, chronology, 2. Dan Mason's letters from 1924 indicate that Wilna and Nan settled down together in Bearsville in June 1924, not April 1925 as she states in her chronology. See letter from Dan Mason to Wilna Hervey and Nan Mason, 14 June 1924, HMP, box 3, folder 11; Knut Hamsun, *The Growth of the Soil*, translated by W. W. Worster (New York: Grosset & Dunlap, 1921), facsimile edition at Open Library, https://openlibrary.org/books/OL14010504M/Growth_of_the_soil; letter from Dan Mason to Wilna Hervey, 8 July 1925, Historical Society of Woodstock (HSW); letter from Dan Mason to Wilna Hervey, 19 October 1925, HMP, box 4, folder 1.

2 Letter from Dan Mason to Nan Mason, 31 August 1926, HMP, box 4, folder 2.

3 Letter from Dan Mason to Nan Mason, 8 August 1926, HMP, box 4, folder 2.

4 Garrott, "People Talked About," 9.

5 Letter from Dan Mason to Nan Mason, 14 October 1924, HMP, box 3, folder 11; letter from Dan Mason to Wilna Hervey, 8 July 1925, HSW.

CHAPTER 9

1 William R. Hervey, Last Will and Testament, 31 October 1924, Queens County, N.Y., recorded 13 November 1925, Book 127, 102, Surrogate's Court, Queens County Courthouse, Jamaica, N.Y. Wilna's $18,883.26 inheritance from her father would be approximately $247,000 in today's money. See measuringworth.com, op. cit.

2 Letters from Nan Mason to Dan Mason, 20 November, 27 November, 30 November 1926, HMP, box 12, folder 7; letter from Wilna Hervey to Dan Mason, 29 November 1926, HMP, box 12, folder 10.

3 Letter from Wilna Hervey to Dan Mason, 9 December 1926, HMP, box 12, folder 10; letter from Nan Mason to Dan Mason, 9 December 1926, HMP, box 12, folder 7.

4 Letter from Wilna Hervey to Dan Mason, 29 November 1926, HMP, box 12, folder 10; letter from Nan Mason and Wilna Hervey to Dan Mason, 21 December 1926, HMP, box 12, folder 7.

5 Letter from Nan Mason to Dan Mason, 7 January 1927, HMP, box 12, folder 8.

6 Letter from Nan Mason to Dan Mason, 21 December 1926, HMP, box 12, folder 7.

7 Letters from Nan Mason to Dan Mason, 5 February 1927, 8 February 1927, HMP, box 12, folder 9.

8 Letter from Nan Mason to Dan Mason, 3 March 1927, HMP, box 12, folder 9.

CHAPTER 10

1 Letter from Dan Mason to Nan Mason, 15 May 1927, HMP, box 4, folder 3; Pietr Hitzig, telephone interview with author, 14 July 2012.

2 David Malcolm Rose, grandson of Ishmael Rose, telephone interview with author, 19 January 2013. Wilna and Nan would be lifelong friends with Ishmael Rose and his wife, Elfleda.

3 Letter from Dan Mason to Wilna Hervey, 14 June 1927, HMP, box 4, folder 3.

4 Letter from Dan Mason to Wilna Hervey, 16 May 1927, HMP, box 4, folder 3.

5 Letter from Dan Mason to Nan Mason, 3 March 1928, HMP, box 4, folder 4.

6 Letter from Dan Mason to Wilna Hervey, 16 June 1927, HMP, box 4, folder 3; "Modernists Show at Woodstock," *Kingston Daily Freeman*, 15 August 1927, 16. One local critic declared: "[T]his picture, Barns, by Nan Mason, I should like to own!" See F. G. Clough, "Third Art Show at Woodstock," *Kingston Daily Freeman*, 7 August 1928, 2.

7 Alf Evers, "Bluestone Lore and Bluestone Men," *New York Folklore Quarterly*, 18, no 2 (Summer), 1962, 96; Anita M. Smith, *Woodstock: History and Hearsay*, 2nd ed. (Woodstock, N.Y.: WoodstockArts, 2006), 25.

8 Letter from Dan Mason to Nan Mason, 14 February 1928, HMP, box 4, folder 4; "Former Movie Actress in Local Film Reels," *Kingston Daily Freeman*, 24 March 1928, 1 (sadly, no trace of this footage survives today).

9 Letter from Nan Mason to Dan Mason, March 1927, HMP, box 12, folder 9.

10 Letters from Dan Mason to Nan Mason, 14 February 1928, 5 May 1928, HMP, box 4, folder 4; "Bearsville," *Kingston Daily Freeman*, 19 April 1928, 3; F. Garner Clough, "Art Exhibit at Woodstock," *Kingston Daily Freeman*, 19 July 1929, 6. Nan had also posed for a small portrait by Wilna's old friend Alexandrina Robertson Harris in the spring of 1926. See letter from Allie Harris to Wilna Hervey, 26 April 1926, HMP, box 2, folder 4. Unfortunately, neither of these portraits of Nan can be located today.

11 "First Art Show at Woodstock," *Kingston Daily Freeman*, 26 June 1928, 2; letter from Dan Mason to Nan Mason, 29 June 1928, HMP, box 4, folder 4.

12 Letter from Aileen McFee to Wilna Hervey and Nan Mason, 25 July 1928, HMP, box 4, folder 8.

13 Wilna Hervey and Nan Mason interview with Jean Gaede; Dorothy Varian, "Thinking of Willie," handwritten eulogy, 3 June 1979, Xerox copy, Blatter Collection, HSW; Mary Reinhard, granddaughter of Maud and Miska Petersham, interview with author, 4 November 2012. Ms. Reinhard was recollecting a later period but her experience seems to have been typical of the enthusiastic hospitality for which Wilna and Nan became famous.

14 Letter from Dan Mason to Wilna Hervey and Nan Mason, 13 October 1928, HSW.

15 Daniel G. Mason, Certificate of Death, 8 July 1929, Office of the Town Clerk, Woodstock, N.Y.

16 Ibid.; Wilna Hervey, memoir supplement: "To Come," unpaginated typescript, HMP, box 11, folder 3.

17 Letter from Dan Mason to Nan Mason, 15 May 1927, HMP, box 4, folder 4; letter from Dan Mason to Wilna Hervey and Nan Mason, 13 October 1928, HSW.

18 Deed of sale from Eugene Shultis to Wilna Hervey, 8 October 1929, Ulster County, N.Y., Deed Book 541, 108, Ulster County Clerk's Office, Kingston, N.Y.

19 Avis Berman, *Rebels on Eighth Street: Juliana Force and the Whitney Museum of American Art* (New York: Atheneum, 1990), 267.

CHAPTER 11

1 Ibid., 309, 310.

2 Letter from Henry Lee McFee to Wilna Hervey and Nan Mason, 6 March 1931, HMP, box 4,

folder 8 (Wilna had sent McFee a tea caddy as a gift and it is apparent that, while grateful, he wasn't entirely sure what to do with it); deed of sale from Elsie F. Buley to Wilna Hervey and Nan Mason, 19 September 1932, Ulster County, N.Y., Deed Book 554, 72–74, Ulster County Clerk's Office, Kingston, N.Y. Elsie Buley was a legal secretary and an employee of Walter J. Miller, attorney and notary public, in whose office the documents were drawn up. Her "sale" to Wilna and Nan of properties they already owned was a legal maneuver designed to position them as "joint tenants" for all of their Bearsville properties.

3 Birkman, "Former Star"; letter from Henry Lee McFee to Wilna Hervey and Nan Mason, 17 March 1933, HMP, box 4, folder 8; program for Carmel Community Players, January 1933, and "Watch Out! Or 'The Spider' Will Thrill You to Death," undated, unpaginated clipping from *Carmel Pine Cone*, Wilna Hervey file, WAAM.

4 Nancy Newhall, ed., *The Daybooks of Edward Weston* (Rochester, N.Y.: George Eastman House, 1961), 273.

5 Henry Lee McFee to Wilna Hervey and Nan Mason, 6 March 1931, HMP; letter from Muriel Pollock to Wilna Hervey and Nan Mason, 8 April 1931, HMP, box 5, folder 4.

6 Garrott, "People Talked About," 9; deeds of sale, from the San Remo Development Company to Wilna Hervey and Nan Mason, 14 May 1929, Monterey County, Calif., Deed Book 354, 298, from Mary Josephine Loomis to Wilna Hervey and Nan Mason, 5 March 1931, Monterey County, Calif., Deed Book 288, 29, from George S. Gould to Wilna Hervey and Nan Mason, 10 April 1933, Monterey County, Calif., Deed Book 363, 1, Office of the Monterey County Recorder, Salinas, Calif.; letter from Dan Mason to Wilna Hervey, 25 October 1927, HMP, box 4, folder 3.

7 Garrott, "People Talked About," 9.

8 Letter from Dan Mason to Nan Mason, 14 June 1927, HMP, box 4, folder 4.

9 "Modernists Show Art at Woodstock," *Kingston Daily Freeman*, 4 July 1927, 16; "New Art Shows at Woodstock, *Kingston Daily Freeman*, 3 July 1931, unpaginated clipping in Nan Mason file, WAAM; "New Art Shows at Woodstock," *Kingston Daily Freeman*, 30 July 1931, 2; untitled, unpaginated clipping from *The Overlook*, 25 July 1931, Nan Mason file, WAAM; "The Third Woodstock Show," *The Overlook*, 8 August 1931, 9, clipping in Nan Mason file, WAAM; untitled, unpaginated clipping from *New York Times* mentioning Nan Mason's "Oliver's Ranch House," 8 August 1931, Nan Mason file, WAAM; "New Art Exhibit at Woodstock," *Kingston Daily Freeman*, 10 August 1931, 7;

"Fourth Art Show at Woodstock," *Kingston Daily Freeman*, 3 September 1931, 2; "Art Notes," *Kingston Daily Freeman*, 29 August 1931, 3; "News of Current and Coming Events in the Art World," *Brooklyn Daily Eagle*, 8 May 1932, E6.

10 "February, by Nan Mason, in the Salons of America at the American Art Galleries," *Arts Weekly*, 30 April 1932, unpaginated clipping in Nan Mason file, WAAM; "New Artists Are Displayed," *New York Sun*, 10 September 1932, unpaginated clipping in Nan Mason file, WAAM; Margaret Breuning, "Art World Events," *New York Evening Post*, 12 December 1932, 11; Anne Smith, art dealer, e-mail to author, 10 August 2012; undated, unattributed clipping likely from *Monterey Peninsula Herald*, Wilna Hervey file, WAAM; Robert W. Edwards, historian of Carmel Art Colony, e-mail to author, 7 November 2013.

11 Letter from Henry Lee McFee to Wilna Hervey and Nan Mason, 17 March 1933, HMP, box 4, folder 8.

12 "Miss Ruth Hart Eddy, 86, Active in Old Bennington," *Bennington Banner*, 16 June 1971, 18; Pat Copeland, "Beach Avenue Once Featured Three Distinctive Homes," *The Sun* [Anna Maria Island], 31 December 2008, 21.

13 Wilna showed her *Portrait of a Filipino* in the summer of 1933 and *Portrait of a Hunter* the following year; see "Woodstock Art Gallery Exhibit," *Kingston Daily Freeman*, 11 July 1933, 2.

14 Birkman, "Former Star."

15 Letter from Caroline Rohland to Wilna Hervey, 7 June 1934, HMP, box 5, folder 8; Wilna Hervey, handwritten notes; "Morristown Property Sold by Trustees," *New York Sun*, 11 June 1934, 39; collection of assorted bills and invoices sent to Wilna Hervey and Nan Mason and apparently unpaid, 1934, HSW.

16 Letter from Aileen McFee to Wilna Hervey and Nan Mason, 13 March 1935, HMP, box 5, folder 8; letter from Eugene Speicher to Wilna Hervey and Nan Mason, 16 March 1935, HMP, box 9, folder 6; letter from Caroline Rohland to Wilna Hervey and Nan Mason, 23 March 1935, HMP, box 5, folder 8.

CHAPTER 12

1 Letter from Frank Capra to Wilna Hervey, 14 October 1935, HMP, box 1, folder 8; "Saturday Society Review," *Kingston Daily Freeman*, 9 November 1935, 7.

2 Letters from Elsie Speicher to Wilna Hervey, 10 January 1936, 9 March 1936, HMP, box 6, folder 8.

3 Letter from Louise Lindin to Wilna Hervey, 23 March 1936, HMP, box 3, folder 6; letter from Aileen McFee to Wilna Hervey and Nan Mason, 8 March 1936, HMP, box 4, folder 8;

letter from Maud Petersham to Wilna Hervey and Nan Mason, 23 February 1936, HMP, box 5, folder 2.

4 Letters from Elsie Speicher to Wilna Hervey, 10 January 1936, 7 May 1936, HMP, box 6, folder 8; letter from Louise Lindin to Wilna Hervey, 23 March 1936, HMP, box 3, folder 6.

5 Letter from Elsie Speicher to Wilna Hervey, 7 May 1936, HMP, box 6, folder 8; letter from Caroline Rohland to Wilna Hervey, 11 June 1936, HMP, box 5, folder 8.

6 Peg Hard, "'Katrinka' of Silent Films," *Kingston Daily Freeman*, 6 December 1948, 6; Kenneth Peterson, President, Lasher Funeral Home, Woodstock, telephone interview with author, 13 November 2013.

7 Letters from Caroline Rohland to Wilna Hervey and Nan Mason, 11 June 1936, 10 August 1936, HMP, box 5, folder 8; "This Coming Week," *Kingston Daily Freeman*, 15 August 1936, 3; letter from George Neher to Wilna Hervey, 3 July 1932, HSW.

8 The author wishes to thank JoAnn Margolis, archivist of the Historical Society of Woodstock, and Emily Jones, archivist of the Woodstock Artists Association and Museum, for their detective work in determining that Kaj Klitgaard was the creator of this tribute to Wilna and Nan.

9 Letter from Caroline Rohland to Nan Mason and Wilna Hervey, 10 August 1936, HMP, box 5, folder 8; deed of sale from Wilna Hervey and Nan Mason to Margaret L. Rogers, 8 September 1936, Monterey County, Calif., Deed Book 498, 12, Monterey County Recorder's Office, Salinas, Calif.; deed of sale from Wilna Hervey to Theresa M. Duane, 3 October 1936, Ulster County, N.Y., Deed Book 584, 120, Ulster County Clerk's Office, Kingston, N.Y.; letter from Henry Lee McFee to Wilna Hervey, 14 December 1936, HMP, box 3, folder 8.

10 "Woodstock," *Kingston Daily Freeman*, 8 September 1938, 10.

11 Mortgage given by Wilna Hervey and Nan Mason to Ulster County Savings Institution, 1 November 1938, Ulster County, N.Y., Book of Mortgages, 437, 23, Ulster County Clerk's Office, Kingston, N.Y.; Charles Hasbrouck and Sons, Well Drillers, to Miss Wilna Hervey, invoice for well drilling, $100.25, 7 November 1938, HSW. They paid for a depth of 58 feet. The amount would be approximately $1,630 in today's money; see measuringworth.com, op. cit.

12 Letter from Wilna Hervey to Leon Kroll, 10 January 1939, Leon Kroll Papers, Archives of American Art, box 2, folder 65; letter from Elsie Speicher to Nan Mason, 22 January 1939, HMP, box 6, folder 9.

13 Playbill for *Summer Night*, 2 November 1939, New York Theater Program Company, Wilna Hervey file, WAAM; Richard Lockridge, "'Summer Night,' Vicki Baum Melodrama, Opens at the St. James Theater," *New York Sun*, 3 November 1939, 24; George Ross, "In New York," *Poughkeepsie Star Enterprise*, 18 November 1939, 6; Gerald Bordman, *American Theater: A Chronicle of Comedy and Drama, 1930–1969* (Oxford and New York: Oxford University Press, 1966), 183.

14 "Miss Santa Claus," *New York Sun*, 18 December 1939, 33; "This Miss Santa Claus Won by a Smile," *New York Sun*, 18 December 1939, 25; "Big Girl (6 Ft. 3—275) Likes Mrs. Santa Role," unattributed, unpaginated clipping, 20 December 1939, Wilna Hervey file, WAAM.

15 Letter from Caroline Rohland to Wilna Hervey, 25 February 1940, HMP, box 5, folder 8; letter from Louise Lindin to Wilna Hervey, 28 February 1940, HMP, box 3, folder 6; United States Census for Town of Woodstock, Ulster County, New York, 1940, online version at Ancestry.com.

CHAPTER 13

1 United States Census for 1940, op. cit. The 1940 census, which lists Wilna as head of household and Nan as her partner, indicates that an unspecified portion of Wilna's money came from "non wages or salary"; letter from Leon Kroll to Wilna Hervey, 12 January 1939, HMP, box 3, folder 3; Denise Sallee, former Local History Librarian, Harrison Memorial Library, Carmel, Calif., e-mail to author, 13 June 2013.

2 Mortgage given by Wilna Hervey and Nan Mason to Ulster County Savings Institution, 25 November 1941, Ulster County, N.Y., Book of Mortgages 455, 328, Ulster County Clerk's Office, Kingston, N.Y.

3 Where and when Wilna met Candis Hall is unknown. A 1931 letter indicates that Wilna is already well acquainted with her. See letter from Molly Pollock to Wilna Hervey, 8 April 1931, HMP, box 5, folder 3; "Niece of Local Man Flies Airmail," *Poughkeepsie Eagle News*, 15 March 1928, 1; Wilna Hervey and Nan Mason interview with Jean Gaede; Pietr Hitzig interview.

4 Pietr Hitzig interview.

5 Deed of sale from Nan Mason to William Maxwell Hitzig and Candis Hall Hitzig, 15 April 1942, Ulster County, N.Y., Book 625, 219, Office of the Ulster County Clerk, Kingston, N.Y.; deed of sale from Nan Mason to William Maxwell Hitzig, 18 July 1945, Ulster County, N.Y., Deed Book 653, 390, Office of the Ulster County Clerk, Kingston, N.Y. Twenty-eight

acres of Treasure Farm went to the Hitzigs in 1942. The remaining 10 acres of the farm were sold to them in 1945. The transactions are under Nan's name as Wilna had conveyed the properties to her for legal reasons that are not entirely clear; letter from William M. Hitzig to Wilna Hervey and Nan Mason, 18 August 1954, HMP, box 3, folder 1; Pietr Hitzig interview.

6 Wilna Hervey and Nan Mason interview with Jean Gaede; Jean Gaede, telephone interview with author, 9 September 2007; David Rose interview.

7 Wilna Hervey and Nan Mason interview with Jean Gaede; Jean Gaede, telephone interview with author.

8 Nan Mason, Dorothy Varian and Wilna Hervey interview with Avis Berman, 22 July 1978. The author is grateful to Ms. Berman for sharing the tape of this interview. Advertisement for Gaylite Candles, Woodstock Playhouse Program, 1942 Season, HSW; Wilna Hervey and Nan Mason interview with Jean Gaede.

9 Wilna Hervey and Nan Mason interview with Jean Gaede.

10 Wilna Hervey, Nan Mason and Dorothy Varian interview with Avis Berman.

11 Berman, *Rebels on Eighth Street*, 451; William Pachner interview.

12 Invoice from Clark S. Neher, contractor and builder, to Wilna Hervey, 23 November 1944, HSW.

13 Letter from Odette Komroff to Wilna Hervey and Nan Mason, 7 February 1945, HMP, box 3, folder 4; Berman, *Rebels on Eighth Street*, 454; letter from Eugene Speicher to Wilna Hervey and Nan Mason, 8 January 1943, HMP, box 9, folder 6; Kenneth Peterson interview.

14 Smith, *History and Hearsay*, 212–217.

15 William Pachner interview.

16 Richard E. Thibaut Jr., "Woodstock News: Pachner Is Named New Curator for Florida Art Center," *Kingston Daily Freeman*, 9 June 1953, 21; William Pachner interview.

17 "Woodstock," *Kingston Daily Freeman*, 16 August 1944, 7; "Health Center Plans Victory Costume Ball," *Kingston Daily Freeman*, 24 August 1945, 3; Wilna Hervey and Nan Mason interview with Jean Gaede.

18 Pietr Hitzig interview.

CHAPTER 14

1 Letter from Fritzi Striebel to Wilna Hervey, 19 September 1946, HMP, box 9, folder 7; letter from Wilna Hervey to Adrian and Sophie Siegel, 4 November 1946, HSW.

2 Letter from Wilna Hervey to Adrian and Sophie Siegel, 3 December 1947, HSW; Wilna Hervey and Nan Mason interview with Jean Gaede.

3 "Woodstock Plans War Memorial on Village Green: Miss Wilna Hervey Named President of Group in Charge; Covers All Wars," *Kingston Daily Freeman*, 26 September, 1947, 1.

4 Ibid.; "Woodstock Club Votes Playground Action for Village," *Kingston Daily Freeman*, 9 December 1947, 1.

5 Peg Hard, "Woodstock News: War Memorial Design Committee Group Meets," *Kingston Daily Freeman*, 4 November 1947, 3; Peg Hard, "Work Started to Raise Funds for War Memorial," *Kingston Daily Freeman*, 14 November 1947, 5; Smith, *History and Hearsay*, 289; Evers, *Woodstock: History of an American Town*, 617; "Wilna Hervey Dies in Fla., Noted Local Artist-Actress," *Ulster County Townsman*, 18 March 1979, unpaginated clipping, Wilna Hervey file, WAAM.

6 "Village Notes," *Kingston Daily Freeman*, 8 January 1948, 24; "Wilna Hervey Is Honorary Head of Memorial Group," *Kingston Daily Freeman*, 25 March 1948, 17.

7 "Woodstock News," *Kingston Daily Freeman*, 17 April 1948, 9; Peg Hard, "Village Memorial Is Dedicated in Special Ceremony," *Kingston Daily Freeman*, 2 June 1948, 3.

8 William Pachner interview; Peg Hard, "Dual Diamond Bill for Memorial," *Kingston Daily Freeman*, 17 August 1948, 2; "Writers, Artists Battle on Diamond in Benefit Game," *Kingston Daily Freeman*, 23 August 1949, 11.

9 "Village Notes," *Kingston Daily Freeman*, 12 January 1949, 11; "Pachner's Three Paintings Feature Gotham Exhibition," 19 January 1949, 18; "Village Notes," *Kingston Daily Freeman*, 24 February 1949, 9; Peg Hard, "Woodstock News," *Kingston Daily Freeman*, 9 March 1949, 22; Peg Hard, "Woodstock News," *Kingston Daily Freeman*, 21 April 1949, 17; "Porcupine Causes Local Animal Uproar," *Kingston Daily Freeman*, 5 May 1949, 23; Peg Hard, "Woodstock News," *Kingston Daily Freeman*, 12 May 1949, 20; Peg Hard, "Woodstock News: Navaho Crafts Sale Draws Many," *Kingston Daily Freeman*, 7 June 1949, 16; "Village Notes," *Kingston Daily Freeman*, 23 June 1949, 30.

10 Letter from Wilna Hervey to Adrian and Sophie Siegel, 3 December 1947, HSW.

11 Peg Hard, "Shotwell Asserts Preparedness Vital in Holiday Speech," *Kingston Daily Freeman*, 6 July 1949, 13. Due to a perceived lack of respect by tourists, who often sat on the base of the memorial to eat and smoke, the bronze plaques with the names of the war dead were removed in 1987 and transferred to the Woodstock cemetery.

CHAPTER 15

1 As late as the census of 1940, Wilna and Nan described themselves as portrait painter and

landscape painter, respectively; Dennis Drogseth, "In Memoriam: Wilna Hervey," unattributed, unpaginated clipping in Wilna Hervey file, WAAM.

2 Letter from Fritzi Striebel to Wilna Hervey and Nan Mason, 2 March 1949, HMP, box 9, folder 7; assorted invoices to Wilna Hervey from *The Little Art Shop*, HSW; Birkman, "Former Star."

3 Woodstock's Art Heritage, 28; letter from Louise Lindin to Wilna Hervey, 22 January 1952, HMP, box 3, folder 7; "Village Notes," *Kingston Daily Freeman*, 23 April 1953, 10; Birkman, "Former Star"; "Woodstock Foundation Announces 1951 Winners," *Catskill Mountain Star*, 26 October 1951, unpaginated clipping in Nan Mason file, WAAM.

4 "Silk Screen Class at Work," *Kingston Daily Freeman*, 28 January 1953, 19. Nan can be seen in the photograph, with instructor Jerry Jerominek demonstrating the technique.

5 "Craftsmen's Guild Offers New Classes," *Kingston Daily Freeman*, 8 January 1957, 5; Sally Perkins, "Enameled Paintings—Wilna Hervey's Discovery Hailed as 'New Art Form'," *Woodstock Record Press*, 6 October 1966, unpaginated clipping, Wilna Hervey file, WAAM; Kenneth F. Bates, *Enameling Principles and Practice* (New York: Funk & Wagnalls, 1951).

6 Perkins, "Enameled Paintings."

7 Ibid.

8 Letter from Fritzi Striebel to Wilna Hervey and Nan Mason, 20 February 1959, HMP, box 9, folder 8. Striebel quotes from a letter she has received from Elsie Speicher.

9 Fritzi Striebel to Wilna Hervey and Nan Mason, 27 January 1954, HMP, box 9, folder 7.

10 Letter from Karin L. Whiteley to Wilna Hervey and Nan Mason, 18 June 1959, HMP, box 10, folder 3.

11 Letter from Karin Lindin Whiteley to Wilna Hervey, 23 September 1957, HMP, box 10, folder 3; letter from Wilna Hervey to Fontaine Fox, 1 February 1957, HMP, box 11, folder 6; letter from Anthony Clark, Toonerville Electric Railway Company, to Wilna Hervey, 23 February 1957, HMP, box 11, folder 6; letter from Karin Whiteley to Wilna Hervey and Nan Mason with attached draft of letter to Frank Capra, 23 February 1957, HMP, box 10, folder 3.

12 Letter from Karin Whiteley to Wilna Hervey, 19 May 1959, HMP, box 10, folder 3.

13 Letters from Karin Whiteley to Wilna Hervey, 8 January, 18 January, 8 February, 2 March 1961, HMP, box 10, folder 3; letter from Wilna Hervey to Norman Cousins, typed draft, 14 October 1961, Collection of Daniel Gelfand, Woodstock, N.Y.

CHAPTER 16

1 Hand-drawn postcard from Wilna Hervey to Bruce Cator, 24 January 1959, Doris and Edouard Blatter Collection, HSW.

2 Deed of sale from Nan Mason to Theodore M. Wassmer and Julia Lund Wassmer, 24 October 1955, Ulster County, N.Y., Deed Book 950, 504–505, Ulster County Clerk's Office, Kingston, N.Y.; Perkins, "Enameled Paintings."

3 Kenneth Peterson interview.

4 David Rose, "Wilna and Roy," *Woodstock Times*, 31 December 2013, 2, online edition at http://www.woodstockx.com/2012/12/31/wilna-and-roy/2/; David Rose interview; Kenneth Peterson interview.

5 "Woodstock Costume Party Is Collossal [sic]," *Ulster County Townsman*, 9 July 1959, unpaginated clipping, HSW.

6 William Pachner interview.

7 Letter from Ruth Hart Eddy to Wilna Hervey, 22 October 1959, HMP, box 2, folder 2; draft of letter from Nan Mason and Wilna Hervey to Ruth Hart Eddy and Alice Gilman, 22 March 1960, HMP, box 2, folder 10.

8 Draft of letter from Nan Mason and Wilna Hervey to Ruth Hart Eddy and Alice Gilman.

9 Deed of sale from Robert E. Knowles, guardian of Marvin Wilson Gray, to Wilna Hervey, 1 June 1961, Manatee County, Fla., Plat Book 1, 216, Office of the Manatee County Clerk, Bradenton, Fla.; letter from Wilna Hervey to John Clancy, Frank K. M. Rehn Galleries records, 1858–1969 (bulk 1919–68), Archives of American Art, Smithsonian Institution, Digital Version of Microfilm Edition: box 7, reel 5857, frames 776–876.

CHAPTER 17

1 Letters from Wilna Hervey to John Clancy, 19 July 1961, 16 May 1962, 13 June 1962, Rehn Galleries Papers, box 7, reel 5857, frames 776–876; letter from Louise Lindin to Wilna Hervey and Nan Mason, 27 February 1961, HMP, box 3, folder 7; "John Striebel, Cartoonist of Bearsville, Dies," *Kingston Daily Freeman*, 23 May 1962, 8.

2 Letter from Louise Lindin to Wilna Hervey and Nan Mason, 27 February 1961, HMP, box 3, folder 7; Eugene Speicher, Last Will and Testament, 14 December 1957, revised 28 December 1961, Ulster County, N.Y., recorded 2 July 1962, Book 48 of Minutes of Wills, 349, Ulster County Surrogate's Court, Kingston, N.Y.; letter from Jean Bellows Booth to Wilna Hervey, 21 July 1962, HMP, box 1, folder 7.

3 Three deeds of sale from Wilna Hervey and Nan Mason to Chemical Bank New York Trust Company, 3 October 1962, Ulster County, N.Y., Deed Book 1130, 545–549, Office of

the Ulster County Clerk, Kingston, N.Y. With the death of Wilna's sister Eleanor, the administration of the Hervey Post Trust had come to Wilna, though it appears she had to fight Eleanor's son, Virgil Brewster, for control. With the addition of Ruth Eddy's help in this endeavor, Wilna and Nan learned how to manage money in a way that surprised even them.

4 "Longboat Art Show Winners Announced," *Sarasota Journal*, 9 March 1964, 8; "Student Show at Longboat Art Center," *Sarasota Herald-Tribune*, 11 April 1965, 12-C; "Prize Winners' Art on Display," *Sarasota Herald-Tribune*, 13 February 1967, p. 7-B; "Top Winners Are Selected at Longboat Key Art Show," *Sarasota Journal*, 12 March 1969, 28; "Paintings Sold," unattributed, unpaginated clipping, possibly from the *Anna Maria Islander*, Nan Mason file, WAAM; Dolores Harrell, past president of The Island Players, e-mail to author, 4 September 2013; programs for plays presented by The Island Players listing technical and production staff, 1961–64, courtesy of Dolores Harrell.

5 "Longboat Art Center Award Winners Told," *Sarasota Herald-Tribune*, 24 February 1964, 10; Perkins, "Enameled Paintings."

6 Letter from Fritzi Striebel to Wilna Hervey, 23 February 1966, HMP, box 9, folder 8; "Longboat Art Center Award Winners Told"; Perkins, "Enameled Paintings"; Birkman, "Former Star."

7 "Longboat Art Show Winners Announced"; letter from Andrée Ruellan to Wilna Hervey and Nan Mason, 2 April 1968, HMP, box 6, folder 3.

8 "Flower Show Winners," *The Islander*, 5 April 1962, 3; "Woodstock News: Guild Announces Annual Craft Exhibit Winners," *Kingston Daily Freeman*, 4 October 1967, 14.

9 Perkins, "Enameled Paintings."

10 Doris and Edouard Blatter, daughter and son-in-law of Hazel Schoeps, tape-recorded interview with Letitia Smith, 29 May 2013.

11 Ibid.; Kenneth Peterson interview.

12 Undated photograph postcard from "Frankie" to Wilna Hervey and Nan Mason, Doris and Edouard Blatter Collection, HSW. According to the inscription, the photograph shows Frankie and his "buddy" George in their U.S. Navy uniforms just before graduation. The two men appear years later in several photographs in an album compiled by Wilna and Nan in Florida, posing at their home with a large painting apparently done by George (they are recognizable in Nan's home movies); postcard from Wilna Hervey to Henriette "Teddy" Reiss, 2 January 1968, Reiss Archives; Birkman, "Former Star."

13 Pia Oste Alexander, telephone interview with author, 14 October 2012; Richard E. Thibaut Jr.,

"Woodstock News: Hervey and Mason Picnic Held," *Kingston Daily Freeman*, 6 July 1955, 3.

14 William Russell, son of the seamstress Clara Russell, telephone interview with author, 17 August 2013.

CHAPTER 18

1 Postcard from Wilna Hervey to Henriette Reiss, 2 December 1971, Reiss Archives.

2 Ruth Hart Eddy, Last Will and Testament, 15 January 1970, Bennington County, Vt., recorded 7 July 1971, 221, 93, Bennington Probate Court, Bennington, Vt. Ruth Eddy instructed that all of her correspondence, papers, memoranda and even photographs be burned upon her death. Aside from two early photos of Eddy on passports, there are no extant photos of her or Alice Gilman.

3 Letter from Andrée Ruellan to Wilna Hervey and Nan Mason, 17 April 1972, HMP, box 6, folder 3.

4 Letter from Fritzi Striebel to Wilna Hervey and Nan Mason, 24 November 1970, HMP, box 9, folder 8; letter from Andrée Ruellan, 23 November 1975, HMP, box 6, folder 3.

5 Letter from Fritzi Striebel to Nan Mason and Wilna Hervey, 6 March 1978, HMP, box 9, folder 8.

6 Letters from Fritzi Striebel to Nan Mason and Wilna Hervey, 28 March 1977, 26 April 1978, HMP, box 9, folder 8.

7 Betsy G. Atkinson, e-mail to author, 18 March 2013. Betsy Atkinson's aunt, Sylvia Snyder, lived on Willow Avenue near Wilna and Nan and knew them well. She was also an executive assistant to the director of Manatee Hospital and was thus the person who telephoned Nan when Wilna died. The exact cause of Wilna's death is unknown. Under Florida law, only family members may request death certificates with cause of death indicated, and none of Wilna's family has survived her.

8 Dorothy Varian, "Thinking of Willie."

9 Capra, *The Name Above the Title*, 35; letter from Frank Capra to Nan Mason, 25 April 1979, Blatter Collection.

10 Wilna Hervey, Last Will and Testament, 9 May 1978, Manatee County, Fla., filed and recorded 12 March 1979, Official Records Book 938, 1518–1523, Manatee County Circuit Court, Bradenton, Fla.

11 William Pachner interview.

12 Doris and Edouard Blatter interview; "Bar Suspends Knowles," *Sarasota-Herald Tribune*, 17 September 1983, 3-B; Dick Peck, "Suspended Attorney Faces Grand Theft Charges," *Sarasota Herald Tribune*, 8 March 1984, 1-2 B; Betty Kohlman, "Lawyer Gets Probation, Fine, in Theft of Clients' Money," *St. Petersburg Times*, 8

January 1985, 1-B. Knowles received two years' probation and community service. He died of a heart attack in 1988. See "Ex-Rep. Knowles, Bradenton," *Palm Beach Post*, 17 May 1988, 5-B.

13 Dorothy Varian, "Thinking of Nan," handwritten eulogy, June 1982, Blatter Collection, HSW.

14 Nan Mason, Last Will and Testament, 24 January 1982, Manatee County, Fla., filed and recorded 2 March 1982, Official Records Book 1022, 3008–3011, Manatee County Circuit Court, Bradenton, Fla. The works that Nan bequeathed to WAAM included pieces by Arnold Blanch, John Carroll, Florence Ballin Cramer, Ernest Fiene, Emil Ganso, Eugenie Gershoy, Manuel Komroff, Jenne Magafan, Henry Mattson, Henry Lee McFee, Caroline Speare Rohland, Paul Rohland, Charles Rosen and Eugene Speicher, as well as paintings and enamels by both Wilna and Nan.

15 Obituary for Nan Mason, *Sarasota Herald Tribune*, 5 March 1982, 14 A; "Artist Nan Mason Dies," *Woodstock Times*, 18 March 1982, unpaginated clipping, Nan Mason file, WAAM; "Graveside Service for Nan Mason Sunday," *Ulster County Townsman*, 3 June 1982, unpaginated clipping, Nan Mason file, WAAM; Dorothy Varian, "Thinking of Nan." Wilna and Nan are buried next to the Speichers and the Rosens, their oldest and closest friends in Woodstock.

Notes to captions

CHAPTER 2

1 The postcard is identified on the front: "Art Department, Adelphi College, Brooklyn – New York." The full inscription on the back of the card reads: "Dearest Chil, This is your Willies art class with our dear old teacher—I just love him, he is just like a dear old child—I spend such happy hours here trying so hard to draw. Dearie don't you think this is a mighty pretty art room! Your loving Willie." It is unknown to whom Wilna originally sent this card. It was not postmarked and was likely enclosed with a letter. Daniel Gelfand Collection, Woodstock, N.Y.

2 "Greenroom Jottings," *Motion Picture Classic Magazine*, 4, 3, May 1917, 58.

CHAPTER 9

1 Letter from Nan Mason to Dan Mason, 23 December 1926, HMP, box 12, folder 7.

CHAPTER 11

1 Miss Eddy's residence was designed in the 1920s by the Philadelphia architectural firm of Heacock and Hokanson. Plans can be seen at the Athenaeum of Philadelphia: http://www.philadelphiabuildings.org/pab/app/ho_display.cfm/56605.

2 Wilna wrote on the back of both photographs. The full inscription on the back of Wilna's photo reads: "To my Valentines Elsie and Gene—If you look right above my head you will see a charming little painting Ethel Magafan gave me. Love from Wilna and Nan." The note on the back of Nan's photo reads: "To our Valentines Elsie and Gene. The radio is at extreme left. The tree was made by Fritzi—with lots of extra trimming by Nan. Those are X-mas lights around the shelves which contain some very pretty shells." Daniel Gelfand Collection, Woodstock, N.Y.

CHAPTER 13

1 Wilna wrote a note to Elsie Speicher on the back of this photo: "Elsie dear—Isn't the house cute in the snow? +you can even see my plants in the kitchen window." Daniel Gelfand Collection, Woodstock, N.Y.

CHAPTER 16

1 Richard S. Thibaut, Jr., "Woodstock News," *Kingston Daily Freeman*, 3 September 1952, 9.

2 Richard S. Thibaut, Jr., "Woodstock News," *Kingston Daily Freeman*, 23 November 1949, 2.

CHAPTER 17

1 Sally Perkins, "Enameled Paintings—Wilna Hervey's Discovery Hailed as 'New Art Form'," *Woodstock Record Press*, 6 October 1966, unpaginated clipping, Wilna Hervey file, WAAM.

List of Illustrations

143 A Ph.D. from Woodstockery College. Hand-drawn document, pen and multi-colored inks on paper, 11½ x 19¾ inches, 1959. Signed by Manuel Komroff and Nat Resnick. Courtesy of Historical Society of Woodstock.

144T The Cottage on Anna Maria Island. Photograph likely taken by Nan Mason, c. 1960s. Daniel Gelfand Collection, Woodstock, N.Y.

144M Nan Mason, *Mullet Fishermen.* Mounted photograph, 10¾ x 13¾ inches, 1952. Signed and dated on mat LR: "Nan Mason 1952." Inscribed on mat LL: "Mullet Fishermen." Courtesy of Historical Society of Woodstock.

144B Wilna Hervey, *Beach Scene.* Enamel on copper, diptych of 4⅛ x 6 inch tiles, n.d. Signed LL: "Wilna Hervey." Daniel Gelfand Collection, Woodstock, N.Y.

145T Nan Mason, *Wilna and Two Dogs on the Beach.* Mounted photograph, 13¾ x 10¾ inches. Unsigned and undated. Courtesy of Historical Society of Woodstock.

145B Wilna Hervey, *Shore Birds at Sunset.* Enamel on copper, diptych of 4 x 6 inch tiles, 1961. Signed LR: "Wilna Hervey." Courtesy of Doris and Edouard Blatter, in memory of Hazel L. Schoeps.

146T Nan Mason, *Zebra Fish.* Enamel on copper, 5 x 3 inches, n.d. Signed LR: "Nan Mason." Daniel Gelfand Collection, Woodstock, N.Y.

146B Wilna Hervey, *Egrets (a.k.a. Feeding Birds).* Enamel on copper, 8 x 10 inches, 1960. Signed LL: "Wilna Hervey" (barely legible). Woodstock Artists Association and Museum Permanent Collection, Bequest of Nan Mason, 1980-13-03.

147TL Wilna Hervey, *Barefoot Fishermen on Wharf.* Enamel on copper, 6 x 6 inches, 1962. Signed and dated LL: "W Hervey 62." Daniel Gelfand Collection, Woodstock, N.Y.

147TR Wilna Hervey, *Anna Maria Beach Scene.* Enamel on copper, 6 x 6 inches, 1963. Signed and dated LR: "Wilna Hervey 63." Collection of the author.

147B Wilna Hervey, *A Day on the Beach.* Enamel on copper, 8 x 5 inches, 1967. Signed and dated LR: "Wilna Hervey 67." Doris and Edouard Blatter, in memory of Hazel L. Schoeps.

149 Franklin Alexander, *Wilna Hervey and Nan Mason.* Oil on canvas, 45 x 55 inches, 1969. Signed UL: "Alexander." Courtesy of Historical Society of Woodstock.

150 A Tale of Two Gardens. Photograph of Wilna amid the Hollyhocks taken by Nan Mason, c. 1970. Daniel Gelfand Collection, Woodstock, N.Y.

151 Flower garden at 112 Willow Street. Photograph likely taken by Nan Mason, c. 1967. Doris and Edouard Blatter Collection, Historical Society of Woodstock.

152L Wilna at work in her Florida studio. Photograph likely taken by Nan Mason, c. 1960s. Doris and Edouard Blatter Collection, Historical Society of Woodstock.

152R Wilna firing an enamel. Photograph by Nan Mason, c. 1960s. Doris and Edouard Blatter Collection, Historical Society of Woodstock.

153T Nan Mason, *Wilna Hervey.* Photograph, 10 x 8 inches, c. 1966. Daniel Gelfand Collection, Woodstock, N.Y.

153B Wilna Hervey, *Picnic on the Bay.* Enamel on copper, 9¼ x 11¾ inches, 1969. Signed and dated LL: Wilna Hervey 69." Daniel Gelfand Collection, Woodstock, N.Y.

154 Wilna Hervey, *The Large Bouquet.* Enamel on copper, 11 x 8 inches, 1967. Signed and dated LL: "Wilna Hervey 67." Daniel Gelfand Collection, Woodstock, N.Y.

155TL Wilna Hervey, *Still Life with Lilies.* Enamel on copper, 8 x 5 inches, 1967. Signed and dated LL: "Wilna Hervey 67." Courtesy of The James Cox Gallery at Woodstock.

155TR Wilna Hervey, *Blue Vase.* Enamel on copper, 7 x 5 inches, 1964. Signed and dated LR: "64 Wilna Hervey." Courtesy of The James Cox Gallery at Woodstock.

155BL Nan Mason, *Calendula.* Oil on cardboard, 20 x 18 inches, n.d. Signed LL: "Nan Mason." Courtesy of Historical Society of Woodstock.

155BR Nan Mason, *Nasturtiums.* Enamel on copper, 6 x 3 inches, 1972. Signed and dated LR: "Nan Mason 72." Daniel Gelfand Collection, Woodstock, N.Y.

156T *Interior with Flowers on a Table, I.* Enamel on copper, 4 x 3 inches, n.d. Signed LR: "Wilna Hervey." Daniel Gelfand Collection, Woodstock, N.Y.

156B *Interior with Flowers on a Table, II.* Enamel on copper, 4 x 3 inches, n.d. Signed LL: "WilnaH." Daniel Gelfand Collection, Woodstock, N.Y

157 *The Tall Girl.* Enamel on copper, 8 x 5 inches. Signed and dated LR: "Wilna Hervey 65." Daniel Gelfand Collection, Woodstock, N.Y.

159 *Wilna in a Wheelchair.* Pencil drawing in sketchbook, image size, 8 x 5 inches, c. 1968. Unsigned. Doris and Edouard Blatter Collection, Historical Society of Woodstock.

160 Nan and Wilna with Hazel Schoeps. Photographer unknown, c. 1972. Daniel Gelfand Collection, Woodstock, N.Y.

A Wilna Hervey
Filmography

Over the twenty-year period from 1916 to 1936 Wilna Hervey made some thirty-seven films. In addition to those listed, Wilna made at least one other film for Sidney Drew and two other films for Johnny Dooley, but these films have been lost and thus the titles are not known. Note that the last of the Toonerville films were being released even as the first of the Plum Center Comedies were making their debut.

Asterisks indicate a film that survives in some form today; a double asterisk indicates a film still on nitrate and in danger of being lost. The major film production companies that Wilna worked with, the Betzwood Film Company and Paul Gerson Productions, are abbreviated as BFC and PGP.

1. *Help!* Drew Comedies, 14 June 1916*
2. *Hearts and Arts.* Johnny Dooley Film Comedies, 1 September 1920
3. *The Toonerville Trolley That Meets All Trains.* BFC, 27 September 1920
4. *Skipper's Treasure Garden.* BFC, January 1921**
5. *Toonerville's Fire Brigade.* BFC, February 1921**
6. *The Skipper's Flirtation.* BFC, April 1921*
7. *The Skipper's 'Boozem' Friends.* BFC, 2 May 1921*
8. *The Skipper Has His Fling.* BFC, 6 June 1921
9. *The Skipper's Narrow Escape.* BFC, 26 June 1921*
10. *Toonerville Tactics.* BFC, 4 July 1921**
11. *The Skipper's Scheme.* BFC, 11 July 1921
12. *The Skipper Strikes It Rich.* BFC, 1 August 1921
13. *Toonerville Follies.* BFC, August 1921*
14. *Toonerville Tangle.* BFC, 5 September 1921
15. *Sweet Daddy.* Schiller Productions,[1] 9 September 1921*
16. *The Skipper's Last Resort.* BFC, 4 December 1921
17. *The Skipper's Policy.* BFC, 19 March 1922
18. *Toonerville Trials.* BFC, 7 May 1922
19. *Toonerville Blues.* BFC, 4 June 1922
20. *Pop Tuttle's One Horse Play.* PGP, 1 August 1922
21. *Pop Tuttle's Movie Queen.* PGP, 10 September 1922*
22. *Pop Tuttle's Clever Catch.* PGP, 8 October 1922
23. *he Skipper's Sermon.* BFC, 15 October 1922
24. *Pop Tuttle, Fire Chief.* PGP, 5 November 1922*
25. *Pop Tuttle's Grass Widow.* PGP, 3 December 1922
26. *Pop Tuttle, Deteckative.* PGP, 31 December 1922*
27. *Pop Tuttle's Long Shot.* PGP, 28 January 1923
28. *Pop Tuttle's Pole Cat Plot.* PGP, 25 February 1923
29. *Pop Tuttle's Lost Control.* PGP, 25 March 1923**
30. *Pop Tuttle's Lost Nerve.* PGP, 22 April 1923
31. *Pop Tuttle's Russian Rumors.* PGP, 2 May 1923
32. *Pop Tuttle's Tac Tics.* PGP, 15 July 1923
33. *Rosita.* Mary Pickford Company,[2] 3 September 1923*
34. *A Pain in the Pullman.* Columbia Pictures, 27 June 1936*

---

[1] Wilna played a suffragette in this film made by the Spanish actor and director Marcel Perez.

[2] Wilna had an undetermined and uncredited role in this film.

Sources

INTERVIEWS

Pia Oste Alexander is a Woodstock artist and the former wife of the late painter Franklin Alexander.

Doris and Edouard Blatter (interview conducted by Letitia Smith) are the daughter and son-in-law of Hazel Schoeps.

Jean Lasher Gaede is a Woodstock author and historian.

Pietr Hitzig is a son of Dr. William M. Hitzig, Sr., and Candis Hall Hitzig.

Rupert Hitzig is a son of Dr. William M. Hitzig, Sr., and Candis Hall Hitzig.

Saartje Hitzig is a daughter of Dr. William M. Hitzig, Sr., and Candis Hall Hitzig.

William Hitzig, Jr., is the current owner of Treasure Farm and a son of Dr. William M. Hitzig, Sr., and Candis Hall Hitzig.

Wheeler Jackson is the son of Bearsville resident Henry R. Jackson.

William Pachner is a noted American artist based in Woodstock.

Kenneth Peterson is a funeral director and president of the Lasher Funeral Home in Woodstock.

Mary Reinhard is the granddaughter of Maud and Miska Petersham, the well-known Woodstock authors and illustrators of children's books.

David Malcolm Rose is the grandson of Bearsville residents Ishmael and Elfleda Rose.

William Russell is the son of Clara Russell, a seamstress who tailored fashionable clothes.

Katherine "Kit" Taylor was the granddaughter of Woodstock artist Charles Rosen.

Eva van Rijn is a Woodstock artist and the widow of artist Edward Chavez.

PUBLIC COLLECTIONS

Betzwood Film Archive, Brendlinger Library, Montgomery County Community College, Blue Bell, Pa.

Frank K. M. Rehn Galleries records, 1858–1969, Archives of American Art, Smithsonian Institution.

George Eastman House, International Museum of Photography and Film, Rochester, N.Y.

Historical Society of Montgomery County, Norristown, Pa.

Historical Society of Woodstock (includes the Doris and Edouard Blatter Collection), Woodstock, N.Y.

Manatee County Courthouse, Bradenton, Fla.

Montgomery County Courthouse, Norristown, Pa.

Motion Picture, Broadcasting and Recorded Sound Division, Library of Congress, Washington, D.C.

Queens County Courthouse, Jamaica, N.Y.

UCLA Film and Television Archive, Los Angeles, Calif.

Ulster County Courthouse, Kingston, N.Y.

Wilna Hervey and Nan Mason Papers, Archives of American Art, Smithsonian Institution.

Woodstock Artists Association and Museum, Woodstock, N.Y.

PRIVATE COLLECTIONS

Daniel Gelfand Collection, Woodstock, N.Y.

James Cox Gallery at Woodstock, Woodstock, N.Y.

Nancy and Lenny Kislin Collection, Woodstock, N.Y.

Robert S. Birchard Collection, Los Angeles, Calif.

Winold Reiss Archives/The Reiss Partnership, Hudson, N.Y.

BOOKS AND CATALOGS

Bates, Kenneth F. *Enameling Principles and Practice.* New York: Funk & Wagnalls, 1951.

Berman, Avis. *Rebels on Eighth Street: Juliana Force and the Whitney Museum of American Art.* New York: Atheneum, 1990.

Bloodgood, Josephine. *With Affection: Personal Inscriptions and the Art of Giving.* Woodstock, N.Y.: Woodstock Artists Association and Museum, 2005.

Bordman, Gerald. *American Theater: A Chronicle of Comedy and Drama, 1930–1969.* Oxford and New York: Oxford University Press, 1966.

Capra, Frank. *The Name Above the Title: An Autobiography.* New York: Macmillan, 1971.

Eckhardt, Joseph P. *The King of the Movies: Film Pioneer Siegmund Lubin.* Madison, N.J.: Fairleigh Dickinson University Press, 1997.

Evers, Alf. *Woodstock: History of an American Town.* Woodstock, N.Y.: Overlook Press, 1987.

Fortess, Lillian (ed). *Woodstock's Art Heritage.* Woodstock, N.Y.: Overlook Press, 1988.

Gaede, Jean Lasher (ed.). *Woodstock: Recollection by Recipe.* Woodstock, N.Y.: Woodstock Township, 1967.

Hamsun, Knut. *The Growth of the Soil.* New York: Grosset & Dunlap, 1921.

Heppner, Richard, and Janine Fallon Mower. *Legendary Locals of Woodstock.* Charleston, S.C.: Arcadia Publishing, 2013.

Hudson, Monica. *Carmel-by-the-Sea.* Charleston, S.C.: Arcadia Publishing, 2006.

Leeds, Valerie Ann, with Tom Wolf and David Belasco. *Along His Own Lines: A Retrospective of New York Realist Eugene Speicher.* New Paltz, N.Y.: Samuel Dorsky Museum of Art, 2014.

Love, Richard H. *Carl W. Peters: American Scene Painter from Rochester to Rockport.* Rochester, N.Y.: University of Rochester Press, 1999.

Peterson, Brian H. *Form Radiating Life: The Paintings of Charles Rosen.* Philadelphia: University of Pennsylvania Press, 2006.

Smith, Anita M. *Woodstock History and Hearsay,* 2nd ed. Woodstock, N.Y.: WoodstockArts, 2006.

Webster, Lawrence. *Under the North Light: The Life and Work of Maud and Miska Petersham.* Woodstock, N.Y.: WoodstockArts, 2012.

Wolf, Tom, and William B. Rhoads. *The Maverick: Hervey White's Colony of the Arts.* Woodstock, N.Y.: Woodstock Artists Association and Museum, 2006.

SCHOLARLY ARTICLES

Eckhardt, Joseph P. "Clatter, Sproing, Clunk Went the Trolley." *Pennsylvania Heritage Magazine,* 18, 3 (Summer 1992), 24.

___ "The Toonerville Trolley Films of the Betzwood Studio." *Griffithiana,* 53 (May 1995).

Evers, Alf. "Bluestone Lore and Bluestone Men." *New York Folklore Quarterly,* 18, 2 (Summer 1962), 96.

Reiss, W. Tjark. "My Father Winold Reiss—Recollections by Tjark Reiss." *Queen City Heritage* (Cincinnati Historical Society), 51, 2–3, 1993, 64.

Rose, David. "Wilna and Roy." *Woodstock Times,* 31 December 2013, 2. Online edition at http://www.woodstockx.com/2012/12/31/wilna-and-roy/

MAGAZINE ARTICLES

"Greenroom Jottings." *Motion Picture Classic,* 4, 3 (May 1917), 58.

Horner, Pat. "The Blue Dome Fraternity—a Niche in Creation." http://woodstockguide.com/musings.html#bluedome (19 March 2014).

Wilde, Wilna. "Inside the Flickerville Bungalows." *Motion Picture Magazine,* 4, 3 (May 1917), 37–40.

___ "Thomas Meighan, Hero of Many Fires." *Motion Picture Magazine,* 13, 1 (February 1917), 111–113.

NEWSPAPER ARTICLES

"Artist Nan Mason Dies." *Woodstock Times,* 18 March 1982.

Birkman, Bernice. "Former Star of Those Toonerville Trolley Comedies Lives on Island." *Bradenton Herald,* 24 March 1965. Unpaginated clipping, Wilna Hervey file, Woodstock Artists Association and Museum.

"Blue Dome in Miami." *Kingston Daily Freeman,* 4 August 1919, 9.

Breuning, Margaret. "Art World Events." *New York Evening Post,* 12 December 1932, 11.

"Brewster Riches Brought Only Woe, Wife Says." *Oakland Tribune,* 12 December 1922, B16.

Copeland, Pat. "Beach Avenue Once Featured Three Distinctive Homes." *The Sun* [Anna Maria Island], 31 December 2008, 21.

"Dan Mason, Famous Syracuse Actor, Dies at Home on Hudson." *Syracuse Journal,* 6 July 1929, 3.

"E.V. Brewster Named in Mystery Suit by His Second Wife." *Brooklyn Daily Eagle,* 25 March 1922, 1.

Garrott, Hal. "People Talked About." *Carmel Pine Cone,* 14 March 1930, 9.

"Graveside Service for Nan Mason Sunday." *Ulster County Townsman,* 3 June 1982.

Hard, Peg. "'Katrinka' of Silent Films." *Kingston Daily Freeman,* 6 December 1948, 6.

"Health Center Plans Victory Costume Ball." *Kingston Daily Freeman,* 24 August 1945, 3.

"Here's What People Have to Say: The Blue Dome Fellowship." *Miami Daily News,* 29 December 1940, 10-A.

Kohlman, Betty. "Lawyer Gets Probation, Fine, in Theft of Clients' Money." *St. Petersburg Times,* 8 January 1985, 1-B.

"Longboat Art Show Winners Announced." *Sarasota Journal*, 9 March 1964, 8.

"Miss Ruth Hart Eddy, 86, Active in Old Bennington." *Bennington Banner*, 16 June 1971, 18.

"News of Current and Coming Events in the Art World." *Brooklyn Daily Eagle*, 8 May 1932, E6.

Perkins, Sally. "Enameled Paintings—Wilna Hervey's Discovery Hailed as 'New Art Form.'" *Woodstock Record Press*, 6 October 1966.

"Porcupine Causes Local Animal Uproar." *Kingston Daily Freeman*, 5 May 1949, 23.

"Prize Winners' Art on Display." *Sarasota Herald-Tribune*, 13 February 1967, 7-B.

"Student Show at Longboat Art Center." *Sarasota Herald-Tribune*, 11 April 1965, 12-C.

"Suspended Attorney Faces Grand Theft Charges." *Sarasota Herald Tribune*, 8 March 1984, 1-2 B.

Thibaut, Richard E. Jr. "Woodstock News: Pachner Is Named New Curator for Florida Art Center." *Kingston Daily Freeman*, 9 June 1953, 21.

___ "Woodstock News: Hervey and Mason Picnic Held." *Kingston Daily Freeman*, 6 July 1955, 3.

"This Miss Santa Claus Won by a Smile." *New York Sun*, 18 December 1939, 25.

"Top Winners Are Selected at Longboat Key Art Show." *Sarasota Journal*, 12 March 1969, 28.

"Two Kindred Spirits Discard Traditions." *Brooklyn Daily Eagle*, 16 November 1911, 6.

"Woodstock Costume Party Is Collossal [sic]." *Ulster County Townsman*, 9 July 1959.

"Woodstock Plans War Memorial on Village Green: Miss Wilna Hervey Named President of Group in Charge; Covers All Wars." *Kingston Daily Freeman*, 26 September, 1947, 1.

ONLINE RESOURCES

Ancestry.com: http://www.ancestry.com

Betzwood Film Archive: http://mc3betzwood.wordpress.com

International Movie Data Base: http://www.imdb.com/?ref_=nv_home

The Maverick Festival, Woodstock, 1915–1931, online exhibition: http://www.newpaltz.edu/museum/exhibitions/maverick/index.htm

Measuring Worth: http://www.measuringworth.com/uscompare/

Newspapers.com: http://www.newspapers.com

Old New York State Historical Newspapers: http://www.fultonhistory.com/Fulton.html

Open Library: https://openlibrary.org/books/

Acknowledgments

At the heart of this book lies a remarkable collection of letters, photographs, art and memorabilia compiled by Wilna Hervey and Nan Mason over six decades. How that collection survived warrants a note of explanation.

Wilna and Nan's aversion to throwing things away serendipitously documented every one of the fifty-nine years they were together. The preservation of the girls' personal archive was not guaranteed, however. At the time of their deaths, their cache of memories was precariously stored in a leaky garage and in the attic of their barn in Bearsville, New York. At their winter home on Anna Maria Island in Florida, there was a similar, albeit smaller, accumulation tucked into every available space.

In 1983 the job of tackling the Bearsville hoard fell to the Woodstock artist Daniel Gelfand. On behalf of his friend, the artist Andrée Ruellan, who had inherited Wilna and Nan's house and barn, Dan and his wife, Jennie, assumed the Augean task of combing through the mountain of debris the girls had left behind. Fortunately for posterity, the Gelfands rescued as much of Wilna and Nan's personal history as they could and ultimately donated reams of historical letters and photographs to the Smithsonian's Archives of American Art in Washington. Thanks to them, the Wilna Hervey and Nan Mason Papers are now available to scholars in our nation's capital.

Wilna and Nan's Florida home went to their friend Hazel Schoeps, who, with the help of her daughter and son-in-law, Doris and Edouard Blatter, also made an effort to salvage important personal items. Like the contents of the Bearsville archive, the Florida trove eventually came into the care of a public institution. Today the Doris and Edouard Blatter Collection, donated in memory of Hazel L. Schoeps, is preserved at the Historical Society of Woodstock.

Without the preservation efforts and generosity of Dan and Jennie Gelfand, Hazel Schoeps, and Doris and Ed Blatter, this book would not have been possible. My heartfelt thanks to all of them. An additional special thank you is due to Dan Gelfand for sharing his own private collection of Wilna and Nan's art and photographs.

The opportunity to talk to the Big Girls' old friends and acquaintances greatly enhanced my understanding of the two artists and their world. I want to express my gratitude to Pia Oste Alexander, Jean Gaede, Pietr Hitzig, Rupert Hitzig, Sartje Hitzig, William Hitzig, Wheeler Jackson, William Pachner, Kenneth Peterson, Mary Petersham Reinhard, David Malcolm Rose, William Russell, Eva van Rijn and the late Katherine "Kit" Taylor for hours of fascinating conversation and the many memories, insights and delightful details that they all were able to supply. My thanks as well to the author Avis Berman for sharing her 1978 interview with Wilna, Nan and the artist Dorothy Varian; Ms. Berman's tape recording of her encounter with the three Woodstock legends only months before Wilna's death is as close to traveling in a time machine as I'm likely to get.

From the very beginning of my research, I received much valuable help from Emily Jones, archivist at the Woodstock Artists Association and Museum. My thanks to Emily, and likewise to her colleague Josephine Bloodgood, former curator of WAAM, for the abundance of material and good suggestions they both provided.

▲ ▲ ▲

At the Historical Society of Woodstock, archivist JoAnn Margolis has been generous with her help. Through JoAnn I had the good fortune to meet Letitia Smith, whose resourcefulness and skilled assistance in tracking down people and information, and conducting interviews when I was unable to get to Woodstock, proved extremely helpful. My thanks to both JoAnn and Letitia.

Renate Reiss, curator of the Reiss Partnership/ Winold Reiss Archives, provided much help in the form of letters, postcards, photos and insights over the years as well as much encouragement and support for this project. *Herzlichen Dank*, Renate!

The opportunity to visit the two Bearsville properties where Wilna and Nan once lived and to step inside their former homes provided many valuable insights into their lifestyle. My thanks to Christopher Anna and William Hitzig, Jr., for their gracious hospitality and cooperation.

In Washington, D.C., I received assistance from Marisa Bourgoin, Wendy Hurlock Baker and research assistant Grace Palladino at the Archives of American Art. At the Smithsonian American Art Museum, Rachel Brooks was extremely helpful. Sim Smiley and Susan Strange provided assistance in retrieving a rare photograph from the National Archives. My thanks to all of them.

In New York City a debt of gratitude is owed to George J. Weinmann for his assistance at the Queens County Courthouse.

In California both Ashlee Wright and Denise Sallee of the Harrison Memorial Library in Carmel provided significant help in finding photographs and documents that illuminated the years that Wilna and Nan spent in Carmel-by-the-Sea. Likewise, Sally Aberg of the Carmel Art Association, Carmel historian and author Robert Edwards, and Helaine Glick at the Monterey Museum of Art supplied me with helpful answers to my various inquiries. Their assistance is much appreciated.

Several individuals in Florida rendered valuable aid in finding property deeds, wills, photographs and old playbills. I extend my thanks to Betsy G. Atkinson and Sylvia Snyder, residents of Anna Maria Island; Dolores Harrell, Board Member at the Island Players, Anna Maria Island; Carolyne Norwood, Anna Maria Historical Society; and Cindy Russell, Historical Records Librarian, Manatee County, Florida.

In Bennington, Vermont, Suzanne Bushee, Registrar for the Probate Division of the Vermont Superior Court, provided valuable assistance.

Rounding up and reproducing all of the illustrations that appear in this book was one of the most complicated of all the tasks leading to publication. I am grateful for the help and cooperation of Tony Adamis, *Daily Freeman*; J. Flint Baumwirt; Edouard and Doris Blatter; Rachel Brooks, Smithsonian American Art Museum; Yuko Ciarametaro, Kaminski Auctions; Jim Cox and Bryana Devine, James Cox Gallery at Woodstock; Daniel and Jennie Gelfand; Thom Gianetto, Edenhurst Gallery; Ani Khachoian, C3 Entertainment, Inc.; Nancy and Lenny Kislin; Mimi Muray Levitt, Nickolas Muray Photo Archives; Harold B. Nelson and Bernard N. Jazzar, Enamel Arts Foundation; Ann Pachner; Renate Reiss, Reiss Partnership; Anne Smith; Derin Tanyol and Eila Kokkinen, Woodstock Byrdcliffe Guild; and Rita Wright, Springville Museum of Art. I also want to express my appreciation to the photographers Ben Caswell, Dara King, John Kleinhans, Michael Richter and Susan Strange for their efforts in accurately rendering the nuances and colors of the many paintings, enamels, prints, photographs and sketches they were called upon to capture.

At Montgomery County Community College in Blue Bell, Pennsylvania, four of my colleagues provided expertise. My thanks to Dr. Lee A. Bender, Professor Frank Short, archivist Lawrence Greene and emerging technologies librarian Jerry Yarnetsky.

Several individuals helped me gain access to some of Wilna Hervey's more obscure film work. My thanks to the film historian Robert Birchard for sharing his rare print of *Pop Tuttle's Movie Queen* and to Jack Hailey, Dennis Millay, Darrell Raby and David Litofsky for making it possible for me to see Wilna's very first film, *Help!*

On a personal note, I want to thank my friend Lynn Holst for permitting me to use her vacation home in Willow during my first research visit to Woodstock in 2011. And I owe a special debt of gratitude to my partner, Brent, for his constant interest, support, and honest feedback during the seven years of research and writing that led to the publication of this work.

Finally, I want to express my appreciation to the publishers of this book, Weston Blelock and Julia Blelock of WoodstockArts, for their careful and intelligent reading of my original manuscript and their many excellent ideas and suggestions during the long process that brought this work to fruition. My thanks as well to their professional associates, editor Jane Broderick and designer Abigail Sturges, for all their efforts on behalf of *Living Large*.

Index

Page numbers in *italics* refer to illustrations.